# Diesels
## — IN DEPTH —
# Classes 24/25

# DIESELS
## — IN DEPTH —
# Classes 24/25

**DAVID CLARKE**

Ian Allan
PUBLISHING

**Front cover**
**Class 25/3 No 25252**
**(D 7602) at Derby in**
**1975.** Peter Hiley

**Back cover:**
**The battery, fuel and**
**water tank**
**arrangements on**
**class 25/1 No D5176**
**(25026).** Author

# Contents

First published 2006

ISBN (10) 0 7110 3171 1
ISBN (13) 978 0 7110 3171 5

Published by Ian Allan Publishing

an imprint of Ian Allan Publishing Ltd, Hersham, Surrey KT12 4RG.
Printed in England by Ian Allan Printing Ltd, Hersham, Surrey KT12 4RG.

Code: 0611/B2

Visit the Ian Allan Publishing website at www.ianallanpublishing.com

# Acknowledgements

This is the second book in the series looking at specific classes of early British Railways diesel locomotives in detail. The Sulzer Type 2s (later known as the Class 24s and 25s) have long been a favourite of mine with their distinctive looks and unusual engine note when idling. From the mid-1960s onwards they became increasingly common in the Shrewsbury area, where I lived at the time, and became the principal power on the Cambrian lines, having replaced the steam fleet, where they remained until the 1980s. They were generally rugged and reliable but the Operating Department regularly gave them loadings which required the driver to work the locomotives really hard, in other words to 'thrash' them unmercifully. This would generate a fantastic noise, much enjoyed by lineside enthusiasts, myself included, but was not appreciated by the maintenance staff who had to deal with the overcooked traction motors!

They were used on all types of traffic and were seen at most locations on the national network (due to their high route availability) and they were long associated with the Scottish Highland main line as well as the Cambrian coast line. Like their steam equivalents (various mixed-traffic 4-6-0s), they were not glamorous, but just got on with whatever train they were asked to pull, only occasionally getting into the limelight when asked to substitute for some more powerful brethren on an express passenger train.

As someone who is also a 4mm scale modeller, I welcomed the introduction of the Class 24 by Bachmann, which although it has some dimensional errors around the curvature of the cab roof, is an excellent performer and I now have seven of them (all with small variations). There were a bewildering number of variants within the 478 locomotives built (151 Class 24s and 327 Class 25s) and it was the collection of material and undertaking research for my models that prompted me to approach the publishers with the idea for this series of books, as I could not find a reference work that summarised all the variants and modifications.

This excellent model has now been enhanced by the introduction of a sound chip by South West Digital (www.southwestdigital.co.uk) which replicates the distinctive engine note exactly, both when idling and under power.

Unfortunately, the revised body style Class 25/3, also by Bachmann, is much less successful, with major errors around the size and shape of the cab front and side windows. It is to be hoped they will produce an improved version as the running characteristics are excellent.

Fortunately, there are a significant number of the type preserved (four Class

24s and 20 Class 25s) with most of the basic variants represented, and I have been fortunate to have driven one of them (No D7671) when on a locomotive driving course at the Midland Railway–Butterley in Derbyshire, close to my home, and I am also the proud owner of one of the works plates from No 25070.

The book would not have been as extensive without the help of a number of people, the largest contribution coming from David Hills, formerly of Derby but now residing in the USA, although the distance has been of no consequence with David running a fantastic website dedicated to the Sulzer Type 2s (http://www.derbysulzers.com). He kindly provided a number of the photos used in the book and helped with corrections to the final manuscript.

A number of Derby residents, mainly ex-Derby Locomotive Works employees, also responded to my appeal for further information and include Peter Hiley who was a pattern maker and amongst his jobs he built the full-size wooden pattern for forming the cabs (and the patterns for the nameplates for the Class 40s named at Derby), Kenneth Oldham who worked in the fabrication shop, Susan Harvey whose father was at the works, and Derek Pinkstone who worked in the diesel engine test house.

Mark Fowler, the proud owner of No D7629, gave me a conducted tour of his locomotive while it was undergoing repairs at Ruddington (the northern outpost of the GCR). The tour included inside the engine compartment, underneath the locomotive, and standing on the roof, which provided a valuable insight into how these locomotives were built.

The amount of time and effort that has to be expended to keep these machines running is enormous and my thanks go to all the owners and groups who maintain their locomotives in operational condition.

**Half-title page:**
An unidentified Class 24/0 outside Derby works diesel test home, where the locomotive would be fully tested before release into traffic. The locomotive has Athermos axle-boxes. *BR*

**Title page:**
Class 25/0 No D5155 (25005) (Darlington 06/1961) is seen in an 'as delivered' condition complete with polished grille surrounds, a feature of Darlington works. None of this batch had steam heating and therefore were not fitted with water tanks. *BR*

# Bibliography

There have been a number of books on the Class 24s and 25s over the years, but none has really done them justice, with most being general picture books without much structure and not good for identifying all the variants. The small number of books specifically on the class is a surprise, given their popularity, but the complexity of detailing the complete history has perhaps put off some authors.

*BR Class 24/25 Diesels* Chris Perkins. Bradford Barton 1982. A small booklet and a good summary of the class.
*The Power of the Class 24* Hugh Dady. Ian Allan 1989. A good selection of colour photos.
*Profile of the Class 24s and 25s* C. J. Marsden. OPC 1981.

Whilst most of the books on the class are now out of print there are a number of excellent websites for the 'Rat' enthusiast (as the Sulzer Type 2s are often nicknamed) as follows:

www.class25.info — This site has extensive details on passenger workings and many photographs.
www.awesome.clara.net/railways — The 'RAT Roadshow'.
www.derbysulzers.com — David Hills' site. Thoroughly recommended.

If we were to compare the BR Sulzer Type 2s (Classes 24 and 25) to steam locomotive equivalents then it would be the Stanier Class 5, LNER 'B1' and GWR 'Hall' 4-6-0s, with all having wide route availability and capable of hauling anything, including express passenger services. These three classes of steam locomotive (and the BR Standard Class 5 4-6-0s) operated over most of the British Railways network and collectively numbered well over a thousand examples. Once the British Transport Commission announced the dieselisation of the network in 1955, a number (174) of 'Pilot Scheme' locomotives were ordered from various external private manufacturers, in addition to BR workshops, in the following power classifications:

– Freight, Type A, 800 to 1,000hp
– Mixed Traffic, Type B, 1,000 to 1,250hp
– Heavy Duty, Type C, 2,000hp and above

The Pilot Scheme locomotives were to be run in service for a period of three years to provide feedback before larger orders would be made. However, even before some of these locomotives had been delivered, the plan was changed and large orders were placed for locomotives, many of them still on the drawing board.

The specification issued for the Type B locomotives was quite broad and was sent out to a large number of companies, with English Electric, Brush, North British, Metropolitan-Vickers and Birmingham Railway Carriage & Wagon (BRCW), as well as BR Derby Works all succeeding in securing orders. Each company was to build locomotives to fulfil this requirement, but with very mixed results. The specification was as follows:

Maximum axle loading 18.75 tons
Maximum speed 75mph

This is believed to be No D5000 as it nears completion at Derby Works. As built, the locomotive had a circular exhaust port which, in this view, is temporarily covered. The cover plate for the water filler (at the top of the steps in the bodyside) has yet to be fitted. The original two-rung step on the side of the bogie is fitted, but later in the build programme this was changed to a three-rung design. *BR*

Multiple working capability (with one crew)
Steam-heat fitted
Locomotive braking – air
Train brakes – vacuum

The manufacturer could decide on the engine and bogie configurations and the method of transmission (electric or hydraulic) as long as it met the overall requirements supplied by BR.

The use of private contractors to supply large numbers of locomotives to British Railways was unusual, with most of the British Railway steam operating fleet having been designed and constructed in the many BR workshops. Where examples of locomotives were built by private constructors the design was normally carried out by the BR works (such as the large number of GWR pannier tanks built by private contractors, but designed at Swindon.) Only Derby of the British Railways works had any experience of designing or building diesel locomotives and of necessity had to buy in the majority of components (engine, generator and traction

motors) from specialised suppliers, and also use the experience of these companies in the design. So when the LMS built Nos 10000 and 10001 Derby worked very closely with English Electric who supplied the engines.

Some of the private contractors already had experience in designing and building diesels for the export market, but, equally, others had little experience of building such locomotives. However, many realised that their traditional markets for steam locomotives would soon disappear and they were keen to use British Railways orders to help them make that transition to building diesel locomotives. For some unfortunately this was too little, too late, such as Beyer Peacock and North British, which both closed down in the 1960s after failing to develop their new diesel fleets quickly enough.

The decision to commission large numbers of locomotives from the private market sent shock waves through the British Railways workshops, but was partially driven

**The premier Class 24, No D5000 as renumbered 24005 at Manchester Victoria, on 30 June 1975. It displays many original features including the split radiator grille, an additional top bodyside grille (five instead of four), original sandboxes and the two-tread steps on the bogie.**
**Modifications include the removal of the valances, the Athermos axleboxes and the shortened water tank. The hand holds to give access to the water filler have been filled in and the works plate removed.** *John Oxley*

Previous page:
Three Class 24s are seen at Euston in September 1964: Nos D5144 (24144) (Derby 11/1960), a 24/1, D5019 (24019) (Derby 7/1959) and an unidentified member of the class in the background. No D5019 is fitted with the Athermos plain bearing axleboxes.
*William P. Power*

The Sulzer Type 2s were built on a production line with the cabs added quite late in the construction process, as can be seen here on a batch being built at Crewe in 1959.
*S. V. Blencowe collection*

by these works being busy with the orders for the BR Standard steam locomotives. Certainly the news that private contractors would be building substantial numbers of locomotives caused a great deal of concern at Derby Works, even though they had secured some of the work. As Derby was little used for the BR Standards (mainly for the Class 5 4-6-0s) and had experience with Nos 10000 and 10001, it was given the task of designing and building the initial pilot order for 20 Type B locomotives.

As the design used many bought-in components the design team would work closely with the contractors providing the components. Derby decided to go with a six-cylinder, four-stroke turbo-charged, medium-speed (750rpm) engine supplied by Sulzer, a Swiss company which had many years of experience with rail-mounted

diesel engines. The generator and traction motors were supplied by British Thomson-Houston (BTH).

One major surprise was perhaps the absence of General Motors of America (whose locomotive division was called Electro Motive Division, or EMD for short) in the British market, as by this time, they were the major supplier to the North American railroads with a series of robust and reliable designs which sold in large numbers. However, they would not license any European manufacturer to make the engines and insisted that all power units were supplied from the USA, effectively ruling themselves out of the competition in the UK. The adverse exchange rate at the time and the need to conserve scarce dollars probably also militated against EMD.

Following announcement of the three categories of locomotive (A, B and C), this was revised to four and became numerical (Types 1, 2, 3 and 4), with the former Type B locomotives now becoming Type 2, the Derby-designed locomotives becoming known as 'Derby 2s' or 'Sulzer 2s' by railwaymen, although when first allocated to Inverness, they were known as 'Derbys' to differentiate them from the 'Birminghams' (later known as Class 26s). Enthusiasts called them 'Rats' which followed on from a comment that no human is ever more than 10 feet away from a rat, and the class seemed to be everywhere on the LM Region.

The design followed the principles of mass car production with components being fabricated as sub assemblies and then coming together on the assembly line. In the case of the Sulzer 2s the cabs were built separately from the rest of the locomotive and were bolted on late in the construction process. This meant that when the locomotives came in for repairs the cabs could be easily detached, which was particularly helpful when repairing accident damage. This also meant a cab did not always go back on the locomotive to which it was previously attached, leading to the different headcode boxes at either end.

**A bogie for a Sulzer Type 2 is seen at Derby Works with the early form of steps (immediately behind the sandbox) with only two rungs instead of the later three. The bodyshell in the background, for another member of the class, clearly shows how they were built without the cabs, which were added as a separate component later.** *BR*

The revised body style locomotives (Classes 25/2 and 25/3) had the cab internals changed, as with the elimination of the cab doors a neater driver's desk was possible. The forward view was also considerably improved. *Author*

Page 12:
A view of the driver's side of Class 24/1 No D5061 (24061) (Crewe 1/1960) as currently running on the North Yorkshire Moors Railway. The nose door shows evidence of duct tape to try to reduce the draughts! *Author*

Page 13:
A view of the second man's side on a Class 24/0 (No D5061) showing the drop-down window and smaller fixed window section when compared with the revised body style. *Author*

The cabs themselves were constructed over a full-size wooden former (which was made at Derby in the pattern making department by Peter Hiley). Even though not all locomotives were fitted with steam-heat boilers, the bodysides were all fitted with hand holds to allow access to the water tank filler and an access hatch for the filler.

The engines were supplied by Sulzer, the first 10 being manufactured in Switzerland and the remainder built under subcontract by Vickers in Barrow-in-Furness. For the initial installation, a number of Sulzer engineers came over to Derby for a few months to resolve any issues with the installation and many of them spent time on the road, trouble-shooting. The Sulzer engine (designated 6LDA28A) was a six-cylinder four-stroke unit with two valves per

The revised body style presented the second man with a handbrake wheel and an air horn, but not much else. This view also shows the revised cab windows with the larger fixed-front section and the movable section now sliding instead of rising and falling. *Author*

cylinder operated by push rods operating the valves. The engine had a single turbocharger operating at 10psi to 12psi above atmospheric pressure and produced 1,160bhp at 750rpm. For ease of maintenance, each cylinder had a separate head and valve chest cover.

Unlike many of the other classes of diesel built for British Railways, the water cooling system on the Sulzer 2s was not pressurised when passing through the radiator, which eliminated the need for frost screens as the radiators were empty when the engine was not running. The cooling water was only pressurised just before entering the engine block. Also, it was not standard practice to use anti-freeze so that many sheds in winter had to employ a 'frost man' whose job it was to run all the engines for a couple of

hours to ensure that the engine blocks did not freeze.

The batteries for the locomotive were located in two trays, on either side of the engine; when safety clamps had been removed, the tray could be pulled out giving easy access and enabling the batteries to be lifted out. The battery trays were revised when the fuel and water tank arrangements were modified with the introduction of Class 25/1.

As part of the programme to keep the locomotive's weight down, the wheels had 16 lightening holes drilled into them, close to the inner tyre edge.

The crew were provided with an electric hob to enable them to cook their own food, this being placed on the cab bulkhead at the No 2 end.

**The first Sulzer Type 2, No D5000, is ready for lowering on to its bogies at Derby Works during construction.** *BR*

The class was built over a period of nine years at three different BR works (Crewe, Darlington and Derby), and one private contractor (Beyer Peacock) and consisted of two distinct body styles. Because of the parallel construction at a number of different sites and manufacturers the locomotives were not put into traffic in numerical order. When the 'new' body style was introduced ('25/2' and '25/3') batches of the 'old' body were still under construction so that the running numbers, the body style and the date of introduction do not necessarily correlate; all very confusing.

Throughout their lives, the opportunity was taken to update and modify the class, both to improve performance and reduce maintenance costs. As first built, they were considerably over weight (by 4.8 tons!) and much effort was spent on trying to keep the weight down, with varying degrees of success. The revisions were grouped into subdivisions of the class and not all of these changes resulted in external differences as many related to the engine, gearing, electronics, generators and traction motors. These can be summarised as shown on the following pages.

The pioneer Class 24, No D5000 (24005) (7/1958), is seen being built at Derby Works having just been lowered onto its bogies. The bond between the glass fibre roof and the metal cab sides on this class was not good, which resulted in body corrosion in later years. *BR*

No D5000 at Derby Works during the next stage of construction, showing the layout of the main components before the roof was fitted. The centre section of the main body roof was a glass-fibre moulding, as were the cab roofs. *BR*

Class 24/0
No D5011 (24011)
(Derby 3/1959)
at Birmingham
New Street on
30 July 1962 is in
as-built condition
and still with a
circular exhaust
port. This was
one of the 10
locomotives fitted
with Athermos plain
bearing axleboxes,
which are identifiable
by their covers.
These could be found
on other locomotives
in the class over the
years as bogies were
swapped around.
*G. W. Sharpe*

## Class 24/0

Numbered D5000 to D5049 (24001 to 24049). The locomotive was geared to give a 75mph maximum speed rating. The Sulzer engine was rated at 1,160hp at 730rpm and the 137BY traction motors supplied by BTH were rated at 222bhp each. The fuel tank capacity was 546 gallons. Most of the first 20 locomotives were fitted with five bodyside grilles on one side which were reduced to four from No D5020 onwards, although Nos D5007 and D5008, for example, had only the four while, later, No 24025 was seen with the additional air intake. The first 19 locomotives also

## Class 24/1

Numbered D5050 to D5150 (24050 to 24159). The engine, generator and traction motors remained as before, but the weight was reduced from 78.7 tons down to 73.0 tons, principally by the elimination of the separate exciter mounted above the generator. Fuel capacity was reduce from 546 to 520 gallons. The major external change came with a train indicator headcode box as fitted from No D5114,

weighed 79.8 tons which was 4.8 tons more than the design weight of 75.0 tons, but from No D5021 this was reduced to 78.7 tons, and from D5044 the weight was further reduced to 77 tons, primarily by reducing the capacity of the water tank from 600 to 450 gallons. Ten of this batch were fitted with Athermos plain bearings to all axles on the bogies and these were distinguished by their different axlebox covers. The first seven locomotives (Nos D5000 to D5006) were originally fitted with split radiator screens, some of these split screens were subsequently fitted to other members of the class.

which displayed the new-style train reporting numbers, a roller blind system as used on buses, but with numbers and letters to indicate the type of train and its destination. These first indicator boxes had plain sides as the locomotives retained the air horns behind the buffer beam. The indicator box was not a separate add-on to the roof but was integral with the cab structure, so when subsequently indicator boxes changed on individual locomotives this was the result of a complete cab swap.

Class 24/1
No D5115 (24115)
(Derby 4/1960)
is seen brand new
at its birthplace
of Derby Works
on 7 May 1960.
This was the second
of a batch of
locomotives fitted
with the first style
of headcode box
and it also had the
modified fuel tank
with reduced capacity
as a weight-saving
measure. *J. D. Pollard*

Class 24/1 No D5134 (24134) (Derby 10/60) in as-built condition with both the
fuel and water tanks with reduced capacity compared with the original Class 24/0.
A Longsight, Manchester, shedplate has been fitted to the nose door as well as a '9A'
painted on the right-hand buffer beam. *BR*

Class 25/0 No 5165 (25015) (Darlington 10/1961) on Leicester shed illustrates the batch of Class 25/0s built with indicator boxes but without the air-horn shrouds. None of this batch was steam-heat fitted and therefore they were not equipped with a water tank. The livery is the early style of blue with double arrows on both ends and the numbers repeated on each side.
*S. V. Blencowe*

## Class 25/0

Numbered D5151 to D5175 (25001 to 25025). The original body style was retained and valances were still fitted; however, the 6LDA28B engine was up-rated to produce 1,250hp at 730rpm. This was done by detailed improvements to the cylinder head and the turbocharging arrangements. The generator was also up-rated and the traction motors were changed to the 137BX type with a small increase in horsepower (to 245bhp). The gearing was also changed to give a top speed of 90mph and indicator boxes were fitted as per Class 24/1. This batch of 25 locomotives was intended for freight traffic and they were therefore not fitted with train-heat boilers and associated water tanks, which meant that the first 15 built weighed 70.25 tons (with 520 gallon fuel capacity), and the last ten weighed 73.25 tons with an increased fuel tank of 620 gallons.

From No D5176 (25026) Class 25/1s had a number of revisions to the body including the side air intakes. The cover for the radiator changed from slats to mesh and the prominent surrounds to the smaller air intakes were eliminated, as here on No 25067 (D5217) (Derby 8/1963). *Author*

The bodyside grilles fitted to Classes 24/0, 24/1 and 25/0 up to No D5175 (25025) had pronounced surrounds and slats to the grilles, as fitted to No D5061 (No 24061). Compare this with the Class 25/1 where the radiator cover was changed to mesh, and the smaller air intakes had revised fitment. *Author*

Class 25/1 No D5183
(TOPS No 25034)
(Darlington 4/1963)
is in as-delivered
condition at
Wellingborough
on 30 July 1963
with the final
arrangement of
battery box, fuel
tank and water tank.
As there was no
valance along the
lower body, the stripe
is positioned a few
inches higher than
previously.
The bodyside
air-intake grilles
have less prominent
surrounds. The cab
doors were also
recessed, as were the
cab window
arrangement.
*G. W. Sharpe*

## Class 25/1

Numbered D5176 to D5232 (25026 to 25082). Although the class retained the original body style there were a number of detail changes incorporated. The cab doors were now recessed and the vertical cab hand rails either side of the door were revised. The cab side windows were revised, with the fixed section now extending further along the window and the movable section now sliding rather than dropping. As before, an indicator panel was fitted to the cab roof but this time the air horns (previously behind the buffer beam) were now fitted on either side of the indicator box in circular housings. The indicator boxes now also had a sloping fairing either side blending into the roof. The valances fitted to the previous batches of locomotives were deleted which resulted in the light-coloured stripe running along the bottom of the bodyside being a couple of inches higher. The speed rating of

90mph was the same as for Class 25/0 as was the 6LDA28B engine. The traction motors were changed, these now being the lighter, AEI 253AY type. Bodyside air-intake grilles were revised with a less prominent surround and they were now positioned behind the bodysides. The water tank filler hatch was now placed on the bodyside, while it had previously been just above the cant rail.

The battery boxes were revised: previously the two boxes were located side by side but these were replaced by a single box under the centre of the locomotive. The revised fuel tank was now located centrally under the new battery box and a water tank (where fitted) was now rectangular and located to the side of the battery box and fuel tank.

A small revision was also made to the sandboxes fitted to the bogies. Previously, they tapered at the bottom, but the revised sandbox had a flat front face.

## Class 25/2

Numbered D5233 to D5299 (25083 to 25149) and D7568 to D7597 (25218 to 25247). The first ten from Derby (Nos D7568 to D7577) and the last 20 from Darlington (Nos D7578 to D7597) used the old body style (the same as '25/1s'); the rest (Nos D5233 to D5299) used a revised body style based on the Class 26. This located all the air intake filters on to the corner of the roof, eliminating most of the bodyside air intakes, and the nose end no longer had provision for doors which allowed for larger windows. The resiting of the air intakes followed a comparison carried out at Inverness with the BRCW Class 26 to evaluate the air quality in the engine room. On Class 24s and 25s, the lower body air-intake filters were found to get clogged-up, reducing the quality of the air entering the engine and thereby reducing performance. Repositioning the air intakes to the roof reduced this problem and also gave more room within the body for air brake equipment. The water filler hatch was on the bodyside as on the '25/1s' (even though only a small number were actually fitted with steam-heat boilers).

**Class 25/2 No D7587 (25237), completed at Darlington 3/1964, was one of the last locomotives built to the old body style and was delivered three months after the first of the revised body style examples had been delivered (No D5233 by Derby, 12/1963). The livery is a little unusual, with the lower body stripe under the window narrower than was normal and the yellow warning panel includes the bottom of the nose doors.** *Pictorail*

Class 25/3 No 25258 (D7608) (Derby 4/1966) is at Willesden in 1978 without a steam-heat boiler water tank and a blanking plate over the boiler air intake. The hand holds to the redundant water filler have been plated over and access hatch for the water filler riveted shut. *G. W. Sharpe*

## Class 25/3

Numbered D7500 to D7567 (25150 to 25217) and D7598 to D7677 (25248 to 25327). The body of the '25/3' was the same as the revised '25/2' but had upgraded electrics. This was an early example of applying solid-state electronics to provide an electronic control system. From No D7568, the locomotives were fitted with an extra compressor for air braking with additional hoses on the buffer beam.

The revised body style was also an opportunity to revise the livery and the locomotives were painted in a two-tone green livery. Class 25/2 No D7507 (25157) (Derby 10/1964) sits at Gloucester Horton Road depot in July 1970. A data panel has been attached and both early and late style sandboxes are fitted, one at each end. The circular exhaust port is still in place, and no water tank is fitted as the locomotive did not have steam heating. *N. E. Preedy*

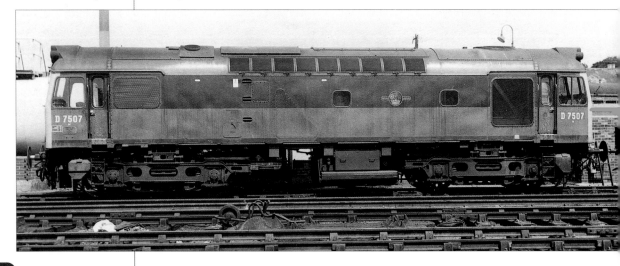

Class 25/3 No D7617 (25267) (Derby 7/1966) at Toton on 7 July 1971 was one of the batch built with a recess under the cab window for the fitment of a tablet catcher for working on Scottish Region. The locomotive is not fitted with a steam-heat boiler and therefore does not have a water tank under the body. The revised version of the sandboxes is fitted. *N. E. Preedy*

Class 25/3 No D7667 (25317) (Derby 1/1967), seen on 14 June 1967 at Temple Mills, was the 1,000th diesel locomotive to have been built at Derby Works and it carried a small commemorative plaque under the double arrow on the No 2 end.
At the time of the photograph, the locomotive was only a few months old and had been delivered in the first version of the blue livery. Unusually for a locomotive allocated to Willesden, it is equipped with snowploughs. It is unfortunate the locomotive was not preserved as a tribute to the loco builders of Derby. *P. H. Groom*

## Class 25/9

In 1985, 12 of the remaining locomotives (all based at Carlisle) were selected from 18 locomotives identified to form a new sub class as '25/9'. These were numbered 25901 to 25912 (and were taken from locomotives in the number range 25262 to 25322). The original pool, based at Kingmoor Yard, was created late in 1985 and involved a dozen Class 25s for dedicated freight traffic in the North West, with the locomotives owned by a BR subsidiary, Railhaul Ltd. All the remaining '25/3s' were load bank tested at Crewe depot, with cylinder peak pressure, electrical machine condition and tyre wear being closely checked. In addition to the 12 selected, there were six spare locomotives all of which were given 'E' exams at Crewe or Carlisle to handle traffic for the Chemicals subsector based at Kingmoor. They were restricted to 60mph to mitigate traction motor problems and were to receive preferential maintenance. They began their duties during December with the renumbering of 25283 to 25904, but the traffic they were assigned to handle diminished rapidly. ICI lost the rock salt contract from Over & Wharton, and sulphur imported through Mostyn Dock ended in 1987. The Speedlink traffic between Dumfries and Carlisle came under critical review and the proposed perlite and sugarstone traffic never materialised. Regional control at Crewe established some diagrams based on Warrington and Garston, involving much oil traffic out of Stanlow. Once this particular 'Sectorisation' plan was cancelled the BRB mandated the '25/9s' be treated like any other Class 25. This sub class was short-lived as all the locomotives were withdrawn by March 1987.

### Summary

The locomotives were not only built as batches by different works, but in batches for particular duties in specific locations, so for example, Nos D5186 to D5222 built at Derby in 1963, were all allocated to Toton for further dieselisation of the Midland main line. These were boiler-fitted and were delivered with small yellow warning panels.

The table opposite explains and clarifies the complex class changes and build pattern.

Class 24/1 No 5056 (24056) (Crewe 12/1959) is seen at Crewe in June 1971 in the final style of blue livery, but not yet renumbered as a '24'. Later style sand boxes have been fitted and most of the valancing is still in place. *N. E. Preedy*

| Running number | Built | Date | Class | Train-heat boiler | Body style | Notes |
|---|---|---|---|---|---|---|
| D5000 to D5004 | Derby | 8/1958–12/1958 | 24/0 | Yes | Original | Fitted with split radiator screens and an additional air-intake grille on one side. |
| D5005 to D5029 | Derby | 8/1958–11/1959 | 24/0 | Yes | Original | Ten fitted with Athermos axle boxes. Nos D5005 and D5006 fitted with split radiator screens. Locomotives up to No D5019 fitted with one additional air-intake grille on one side. |
| D5030 to D5049 | Crewe | 6/1959–4/1960 | 24/0 | Yes | Original | |
| D5050 to D5065 | Crewe | 11/1959–2/1960 | 24/1 | Yes | Original | |
| D5066 to D5075 | Derby | 2/1960–3 /1960 | 24/1 | Yes | Original | |
| D5076 to D5093 | Crewe | 2/1960–7/1960 | 24/1 | Yes | Original | |
| D5094 to D5113 | Darlington | 2/1960–1/1961 | 24/1 | Yes | Original | |
| D5114 to D5150 | Derby | 4/1960–2/1961 | 24/1 | Yes | Original | Headcode boxes fitted to cab roof. Nos D5114 to D5132 delivered with recess in cab side for tablet catcher fitment when used in Scotland. |
| D5151 to D5175 | Darlington | 4/1961–4/1962 | 25/0 | No | Original | Headcode boxes fitted to cab roof. |
| D5176 to D5185 | Darlington | 1/1963–5/1963 | 25/1 | Some only | Original | Headcode boxes plus air horn covers either side of headcode box. No valances from new. Nos D5179 to D5182 not boiler fitted. Revised sandboxes, cab doors and cab windows. Delivered in green with small yellow warning panels. |
| D5186 to D5222 | Derby | 3/1963–9/1963 | 25/1 | Yes | Original | Delivered in green with small yellow warning panel. |
| D5223 to D5232 | Darlington | 7/1963–11/1963 | 25/1 | Yes | Original | Delivered in green with small yellow warning panels. |
| D5233 toD5299 | Derby | 12/1963–10/1964 | 25/2 | No | Revised | Nos 5233 to 5237 had steam-heat boilers, the rest of this batch did not. Delivered in two-tone green and small yellow warning panels. |
| D7500 to D7567 | Derby | 1964–1966 | 25/2 | No | Revised | Delivered in two-tone green and small yellow warning panels. |

| Running number | Built | Date | Class | Train-heat boiler | Body style | Notes |
|---|---|---|---|---|---|---|
| D7568 to D7577 | Derby | 10/1963–12/1963 | 25/2 | Yes | Original | Derby used the old body style for the first ten Class 25/2s before adopting the new body for the rest. Delivered in green with small yellow warning panels. |
| D7578 to D7597 | Darlington | 12/1963– 8/1964 | 25/2 | Yes | Original | The last of the old body style delivered some eight months after the first of the new style was delivered! Delivered in green with small yellow warning panels. |
| D7598 to D7623 | Derby | 2/1966–10/1966 | 25/3 | No | Revised | Nos D7611 to D7623 built with cab side recess for tablet catcher when working on the Scottish Region. Delivered in two-tone green and small yellow warning panels. |
| D7624 to D7659 | Beyer Peacock | 10/1965–7/1966 | 25/3 | No | Revised | Delivered in two-tone green and small yellow warning panel. |
| D7660 to D7677 | Derby | 12/1966–5/1967 | 25/3 | No | Revised | Delivered in two-tone green and small yellow warning panel. The last 18 locomotives (Nos D7660 to D7677) delivered in blue livery, two with small yellow warning panels, the remainder with full yellow ends. |

**Class 24/0 No D5000 (24005) (Derby 8/1958) was delivered in an unusual livery with a thin pale-blue band at waist level, displayed here at Hither Green in April 1964. No other members of the class were so treated and D5000 retained this one-off livery until repainted blue.** *R. A. Panting*

# MODIFICATIONS

Class 24/0 No 24025 (D5025) (Derby 10/1959) awaits its fate on the scrap line in Swindon, fitted with a split radiator grille as originally found only on the first six locomotives, but which subsequently were re-used on other members of the class (24006, 24025 and 24134). The rust patch on the door shows where the works plate had been fixed. The cab side handrails are white and the revised style of sandboxes are fitted. This view shows the flush doors fitted to Nos D5000-D5175.
*Peter Hiley*

## Split radiator screens

The first five locomotives (Nos D5000 to D5004) were fitted with the radiator grilles split in two with a horizontal bar across the middle. As many of the components on the class were considered interchangeable, these grilles found their way on to other locomotives and the following were fitted with at least one of these grilles when they were withdrawn: Nos 24006 (1975), 24025 (1976) and 24134 (1976).

At least two of the original locomotives retained these original grilles until withdrawal: Nos 24003 (1976) and D5001 (1975). One locomotive, No 24001, had had at least one of the original screens replaced with the more usual type when withdrawn in 1975, and No 24005 (D5000) was still fitted with these grilles in 1975 when in blue livery.

Class 24/0 No D5007 (24007) (Derby 2/1959) in as-built condition complete with early-style two-rung bogie steps, and the first version of the original style of sandbox is fitted fuel and water tanks. *Sam Lambert*

Class 24/0 No D5018 (24018) (Derby 6/1959) is seen at Watford on 13 January 1961 showing the Athermos axleboxes as fitted to 10 members of the class. The locomotive is also fitted with five small air intakes on the top row of grilles, compared with the more usual four. The fuel and water tanks remain as built. *R. K. Evans*

## Bodyside air intakes

When built, Nos D5000 to D5019 had an additional air intake on the top row on one side. Nos D5008 and D5009 were not so fitted and had four air intakes. However, other examples were seen subsequently with this additional air intake, eg No 24025.

## Athermos axleboxes

Ten locomotives from the first batch (Nos D5010 to D5019) were fitted with Athermos plain bearing axleboxes for comparison with the standard roller bearing type fitted to the rest of the class, but these were not deemed successful enough to replace the standard roller bearings. As bogies were swapped between locomotives these axleboxes were seen on other locomotives, eg Nos D5064 (in 1971) and D5000 (in 1970 and also in 1974, after being renumbered 24005).

## Bogie steps

The first batch of locomotives had a bogie step that had only two rungs and was comparatively wide. Subsequently the step was revised to three rungs and the ladder itself became narrower. The first 36 loco- motives (Nos D5000 to D5035) were certainly fitted with the original design. This early version of the bogie steps appears to have been retained by many locomotives throughout their lives, but some acquired the modified three-rung variety.

## Welded-up end doors

The end doors to enable multiple working were hardly ever used and were a source of considerable draughts in the cab; not a good idea when working in Scotland in mid-winter. The process of welding up or replacing the doors appears to have been a gradual one. The first stage involved metal strips covering the joints on the doors before having the doors replaced later by a steel plate welded into the aperture and made good. This usually meant that all clips, hinges and brackets were removed. The process of replacing the end doors took place over a long period, with No 25046 having its doors removed as late as 1980 when overhauled at Glasgow Works. A small number of locomotives retained their nose doors until withdrawal, including Nos 24015 and 25029.

Class 25/2, No 25246 (D7596) (Darlington 7/1964) shows the Glasgow style of livery at Polmadie on 9 July 1978, with the number on the bodyside and the blue stars on the front located towards the centre of the locomotive. The nose doors have been plated over, as have the hand holds for accessing the water filler. The shedcode can be seen below the data panel. *G. W. Sharpe*

Class 24/0 No 24009 (D5009) (Derby 3/1959) at Eastfield depot, Glasgow, on 11 June 1975 displays evidence of a recent visit to Glasgow Works. When welding up the nose doors the headcode discs and lights had been centred and the loco number has been painted on the bodyside. The location of the blue stars closer to the centre of the body was also a Glasgow trademark, but the yellow warning panel covering the front roof guttering is more unusual. The original bogie step with two rungs is still fitted.
*N. E. Preedy*

For the locomotives not fitted with headcode boxes, a visual indicator that the welding up of the doors had been carried out at Glasgow Works was the practice of placing the headcode discs in the centre of the door, rather than the more usual off-centre position. Examples included Nos 24005, 24007, 24009 and 24072.

Class 24/1 No 5126 (No 24126) (Derby 7/1960) shows the early modifications applied to the nose doors, with a metal strip having been applied to cover the gaps. A 60A, Inverness, shedplate has been fitted, as have a pair of spotlights for operating in Scotland. A snowplough has also been fitted. The two blue stars are located close to the centre of the locomotive, indicating it has been overhauled at Glasgow Works.
*Ian Allan Library*

## Exhaust ports

The class was originally built with a circular exhaust port in the roof, close to the No 2 end (the end furthest from the radiator intake). The space between the exhaust port and the turbo-charger was filled with an expansion chamber which acted as a silencer. However, the expansion box was also used to vent oil fumes which allowed oil to collect in the silencer box and at various times the silencers caught fire, causing damage to the surrounding bodywork.

In August 1961 No D5089 and D5085 were observed on the Churnet Valley line (not far from Derby Works) in connection with noise level tests for a revised exhaust (eliminating the expansion chamber), the only silencing being provided by the turbo-charger. In October 1961, Nos D5053 and

Class 24/0 No D5032 (24032) (Crewe 7/1959) passes Euston Carriage Sidings signalbox as it descends Camden Bank on 31 August 1964 with the 7.14am Bletchley–London Euston train. On the right, sister loco No D5024 (24024) (Derby 10/1959) sets empty suburban stock back into the carriage sheds. The two locomotives have different styles of exhaust ports, with No D5032 having the revised rectangular type while No D5024 has the original circular pattern port located closer to the cab (due to the silencer). Both locomotives display the small yellow warning panel with rounded corners.
*Brian Stephenson*

D5069 had their round exhaust ports sealed and replaced by a new rectangular port cut immediately above the engine's turbo-charger. The work was carried out at Finsbury Park shed. The revised exhaust port was located further down the roof towards the centre of the locomotive, and this became the standard for all BR Sulzer Type 2s. However, it was to take some time for all members of the class to be converted, and, for example, No 5082 still had its original port in 1973. In the transition between the two types the following variants have been observed:

– Original exhaust port left in place, but with replacement exhaust further down the body.

– Original port plated over with a circular plate and revised exhaust further down the body.

Strangely, some new-build locomotives continued to appear with the old arrangement, so that the locomotives in the new body style built at Derby in 1966 were out-shopped with the earlier style ports. Most locomotives were fitted with the revised arrangements by the late 1960s.

For the revised body style locomotives fitted with a circular port, this was located closer to the centre of the locomotive and when this was replaced by a rectangular port this was only a few feet away from the original port, and no silencer was fitted.

# Fuel and water tanks

Throughout their lives, the style, capacity and positioning of the fuel and water tanks were constantly being changed, usually in an attempt to keep the overall weight of the locomotive down without affecting its operating efficiency and range.

As with many changes to the class, some of the modifications applied to new batches were subsequently applied to previous examples, but there was little consistency in this process. When first built, the Class 24s exceeded their design weight and the class was subject to various schemes to reduce this. Many of the first batch when allocated to the Southern Region had the steam-heat boiler water tanks removed. This was done at Eastleigh Works in February 1959 on the instructions from the Chief Civil Engineer. This decision was reversed in January 1960 and the locomotives were sent back to Derby to have their tanks refitted. This

caused some consternation to the staff at Derby as the locomotives had left the works with water tanks and had reappeared some time later with them missing! In terms of positioning, the fuel tank was at the radiator (No 1) end and the water tank was at the boiler grille end. The principle of trying to reduce the weight by modifying the water tanks however carried on with various modifications made as follows:

## Class 24. Nos D5000 to D5049 (24001 to 24049), as built

In these examples the fuel and water tanks were wrapped around the two centrally located battery boxes with the break between the fuel and water tank (under the batteries) being off-centre (the fuel tank was externally longer). The water tank had 600 gallons capacity and the fuel tanks had a capacity of 546 gallons. From No D5044 the water tank capacity was reduced to 450 gallons.

A close-up of a gauge fitted to a Class 24 water tank. Similar gauges were sometimes fitted to fuel tanks, but this seems to have been a fairly random affair, with many tanks not being fitted with external gauges.
*Author*

Class 24/1 No D5085 (24085) (Crewe 5/1960) is depicted at Willesden on 30 April 1966 and shows the first attempt at modifying fuel and water tanks to reduce weight. This batch of locomotives, Nos D5050 to D5129, had the vertical section of the fuel tank lowered in height, which reduced the fuel capacity by 26 gallons. The fuel tank was always towards the radiator (No 1) end of the locomotive. *P. H. Groom*

This is the original fitment of fuel and water tanks as installed on Nos D5000 to D5049 (Class 24/0). The water tank gauge is a later addition and the valance has been removed on this example. No gauge is fitted to the fuel tank. *Author*

## Class 24/1
### Nos D5050 to D5120 (24050 to 24120)
The first attempt at reducing the weight came with this batch of locomotives when the vertical section of the fuel tank was reduced, and no longer reached up to the frames. This seemed an unusual way to reduce weight as this brought the fuel capacity down to 520 gallons; it would have been expected that the water tank capacity would have been reduced instead.

## Class 24/1
### Nos D5121 to D5150 (24121 to 24150)
For this batch, the design of the water tank was reduced with the horizontal section decreased in length creating a gap between the fuel and water tanks. This batch of locomotives also included the Gateshead-allocated locomotives which were dedicated to the Tyne Dock to Consett iron ore workings and were delivered with steam-heat boilers and water tank, those allocated to the Consett workings having the water tank and boiler removed after delivery. Subsequently, many of this batch of locomotives had gauges fitted to both the fuel and water tanks, or sometimes just to one of the tanks.

**Class 24/1 No D5147 (24147) (Derby 12/1960), at Carnforth on 28 July 1968, was one of the Class 24/1s subsequently fitted with modified headcode boxes with winged extensions but no air-horn covers. This batch of locomotives (Nos D5121 to D5150) was built with revised fuel and water tanks with reduced capacities. It is in green livery with full yellow ends, but still has the original circular exhaust port.**
*G. W. Sharpe*

**From No D5050 to D5120, a revised fuel tank was fitted with a reduction in capacity (and therefore weight) and can be distinguished by the vertical section of the tank no longer reaching the underframe.** *Author*

### Class 25/0
### Nos D5151 to D5175 (25001 to 25025)

The Class 25s started where the Class 24 left off, with a fuel tank that did not reach up to the frames on the vertical surface.

### Classes 25/1, 25/2 and 25/3
### Nos D5176 to D7677 (25026 to 25327)

The first of the '25/1s' received the final variation with a completely new arrangement of fuel and water tanks. In this case the battery boxes were also revised to a single tray per side (formerly two trays per side) and the fuel tanks were located underneath these. The water tank (where fitted) was more rectangular and located to one side (at the boiler grille side). As with the earlier examples, some were fitted with gauges and some not.

The battery, fuel and water tank arrangements were revised from the start of Class 25/1, No D5176 (25026) onwards. The fuel tank was positioned centrally under the (single) battery box and, when fitted, the water tank sat to the right of the fuel tank, with hand holds to access the water filler located behind a hinged flap on the bodyside.

The majority of Class 25/2s and 25/3s were not built with steam-heat boilers and therefore did not have water tanks. This view shows the space adjacent to the revised fuel and single battery box, as fitted to the later-style locomotives.
*Author*

Once the various batches had been delivered they were subsequently modified so locomotives fitted with the original fuel or water tanks could be fitted with some of the modified versions, very much a mix-and-match arrangement. When a locomotive entered works it was completely stripped down, with all the removed components sent for refurbishment to the various sections in the works. During the rebuilding process the first available component would be fitted, hence locomotives exchanged cabs, sandboxes, fuel and water tanks.

The batteries were originally stored in two compartments under the middle of the locomotive, but from No D5176 (25026) (Darlington 1/1963), the battery arrangements were revised (along with the fuel and water tanks) to a single compartment which could be slid out for access. *Author*

Class 24/1 No D5100 (24100) (Darlington 6/60) runs through Church Fenton in September 1966 on a freight service. The fuel tank has been reduced in capacity (by lessening the height) and a replacement cover plate for the water filler can be seen on the curve of the roof. The cab hand rails are not painted white but are either green or in a natural steel finish. *G. W. Sharpe*

A detailed view of No 24037 at Chester in 1976. Later sandboxes are fitted as is the later style of three rung steps. The valancing has been removed to the right of the driver's door. The data panel is seen below the builder's plate.
*David Cousins*

## Boiler room grille covers

All the locomotives built were fitted with an intake to provide air for the steam-heat boiler, even though half of the class was built without this steam heat feature and its associated equipment. The air intake consisted of a grille panel two-thirds of the way up the bodyside, but experience with members of the class operating in the Highlands, of drawing excessive quantities of cold air into the boiler compartment, led to the development of a blanking plate to replace the grille. Later, this blanking plate was modified with five slots to allow a lower volume of air into the train-heat boiler compartment, although No D5127 was seen with a plate with four slots in 1966 and 1974 (as No 5127 in blue). Examples seen with five slots include Nos 5121 (1974) and 5126 (1971).

The solid blanking plate appeared on most of the class, even those originally fitted with a train-heat boiler. Many locomotives originally fitted with steam-heat boilers had them removed and those that retained the fitment rarely found themselves on a passenger train that required a working boiler.

Subsequently, rather than a separate blanking plate, the boiler room air intake was sheeted over flush with the bodysides when the locomotives were in works. Examples include Nos 25104, 25111 and 25161. There were two methods for this sheeting over: the simple way was to skin over the opening; the other was to resheet the whole panel from the frame level up to the cant rail.

## Valance removal

Locomotives up to No D5175 were built with a valance between the bodyside and the bogie. From No D5176 onwards this fitting was deleted when the locomotives were built. Locomotives prior to this batch which were built with the valance had them removed, but this took several years to effect. In some cases, the valance was removed in sections so that for a period of time a locomotive would have gaps in it which was visually very unsatisfying as it gave a shabby appearance. Whilst most locomotives had the valances removed, a number of Class 24s retained them until withdrawal.

## Sandboxes

The original sandboxes fitted to the leading edge of the bogies had the front face chamfered-in halfway down. From No D5176 (25026) the shape of the sandboxes was changed with a flat vertical face. Given that the batches were delivered out of sequence and the numerical order was not the same as the date of introduction, it is not clear if other batches around the same time were fitted with the old or revised style of box. Over time, locomotives fitted with the original style of sandbox would acquire the new style ones and vice versa, and there are many examples of both types being fitted to the same locomotive. As the bogies were not always interchangeable (because of differing traction motors), it is assumed that the sandboxes were detached from the bogies in works and would therefore get mixed up when refitted.

The first style of sandbox was fitted to Nos D5000 to D5175. It was quite complex in shape with many sloping surfaces and was subsequently revised. Both styles of sandboxes could be seen on all members of the class following overhaul, including both styles on the same locomotive. *Author*

Class 25/1 No 25057 (D5207) (Derby 6/1963) is seen at Perth in June 1981. The nose doors have been welded up but the clips have been retained. The grille cover for the radiator is missing and later-style sandboxes are fitted. The hole in the centre of the door near the bottom is for the communication cable when working Royal Trains. *G. W. Sharpe*

The sandboxes were revised from No D5176 (No 25026) (Darlington 1/1963) with more flat surfaces than the previous design. However, the two types were interchangeable so that both could be seen on the same locomotive. This is on No 25067 (D5217). *Author*

## Brake tenders

When diesels were first being introduced, many freight trains were still unfitted and therefore relied on the brake capacity of the locomotive and brake van to stop the train. When compared with its steam counterparts a diesel was very often lighter and with fewer braked wheels (a steam locomotive also having brakes on the tender wheels) and it become more common for trains to have problems with stopping. As an example a number of Class 24/25s were withdrawn following runaway accidents. To assist the diesel fleets, a number of depots which were responsible for working unfitted freight trains were allocated brake tenders.

These were introduced between 1961 and 1964 and in total, 122 were produced at a number of works, both BR (Darlington, Stratford and Cowlairs) and private companies (Marcroft, Central Wagon and Standard Wagon) and reused second-hand coach bogies (either Gresley design or ex-LMS).

At first, the brake tenders were placed in front of the locomotive, but following some complaints from the rail unions, these were subsequently coupled behind the locomotive. Toton in the East Midlands, which covered a large number of colliery workings with unfitted freight trains, used a considerable number of brake tenders, as did Gateshead depot.

Class 24/1 No D5112 (24112) (Darlington 12/1960) propels a brake tender fitted with redundant Gresley-style coach bogies at ICI Billingham on 19 March 1963. Following the example of the locomotive, the brake tender also has a small yellow warning panel. The chemical wagons were specifically designed for the conveyance of ICI chemicals. *BR*

Class 24/1 No 5123 (24123) (Derby 6/1960) displays many of the modifications applied to the Class 24/1s allocated to the Highland main line, including a blanking plate to the air intake for the steam-heat boiler which has five slots, and two spotlights on the nose. A recess has been cut for the tablet catcher, but this is not in place. The early-style sandboxes are fitted and the hand rails appear to have been painted blue.
*Ian Allan Library*

## Tablet catchers

A batch of locomotives was built (Nos D5114 to D5132) (24114 to 24132) specifically for service on the old Highland main line in Scotland, which had long single-line sections. They were delivered with a recess on one cab under the driver's window (on each side) to allow the fitment of a tablet catcher. The recess in the cab side also meant that the drop-down window for the driver had to be replaced by a sliding version. These tablet catchers were later removed and only Nos D5116 and D5117 were observed with them fitted when carrying blue livery.

A batch of the revised body style locomotives also received the tablet catcher recess, Nos D7611 to D7623 (25261 to 25273) for service in Scotland. Following the removal of the tablet catchers, many locomotives had the recess sheeted over.

Class 24/1 No 5126 (24126) (Derby 7/1960) shows off its tablet catcher at Inverness on 10 April 1971. The boiler air-intake blanking plate has been modified with five slots, and in common with other Inverness-based locomotives, it also has two spotlights on the nose.
*D. L. Percival*

Class 24/1 No D5129 (24129) (Derby 9/1960) couples up to a PMV at Kyle of Lochalsh on 15 July 1968 showing an early example of blue livery, but retaining the 'D' number on the cab side. The locomotive has been fitted with a tablet catcher and spotlights for use on the Highland main line. The sandboxes are of the early type and a shedplate has been fitted to the nose. The valances have been removed, and a blanking plate (without air slots) has been fitted over the boiler air intake. *G. W. Sharpe*

Class 24/1 No 24116 (D5116) (Derby 5/1960) at Haymarket shed on 19 April 1976, showing how the recesses for the two spot lamps have been covered over by circular plates after the lamps have been removed. The headcode box has a non-standard Perspex cover with prominent bolt heads and the nose doors have been welded up. *Gavin Morrison*

## Front headlamps

The batch of locomotives, Nos D5114 to D5132 (24114 to 24132), allocated initially to the Highland main line, were fitted with two spotlights in the centre of the nose to give approach warning to users of unprotected level crossings. The first locomotives so equipped were Nos D5127 and D5131, followed by Nos D5114 to D5132. Subsequently, some of these had the lights removed and a rectangular or circular blanking plate placed over the recess, an example being No 24125.

There is no evidence that the later batch with the revised bodywork allocated to the Highland main line, Nos D7611 to D7623, which were fitted with tablet catchers, were ever fitted with spotlights.

From D5000 to D5175 the steam-heat boiler water tank filler located under a hatch on the curve into the roof (the cant rail) and was accessed by hand holds on the bodyside. Later, when the steam-heat boilers were no longer required, these hand holds were plated over. *Author*

From No D5176 (Class 25/1) onwards, revised arrangements for filling the steam-heat boiler water tank were made. With the filler hatch moved from the cant rail to the bodyside with a hinged door providing access. These hatches were fitted to all Class 25/1s, 25/2s and 25/3s, even if they were not fitted with steam-heat equipment. Many locomotives later had these hinged doors replaced with a fixed plate when there was no longer a need to fill the water tank. *Author*

## Steam-heat water filler cap and hand holds

When originally built, the filler for the steam-heat boiler water tank was located in the roof (just above the cant rail) and there were hand holds cut into the bodyside to allow the second man to gain access to the filler. With the removal of the steam-heat boiler and water tanks many of the class had the hand holds plated over.

The curved access cover plate for the water tank filler, which matched the roof profile in the original design, appears to have been taken off almost immediately the class was introduced, and it is rare to find photographs of locomotives with this cover plate *in situ*.

From No D5176 onwards, all the '25/1s', '25/2s' and '25/3s' had the water filler moved to the bodyside, adjacent to the hand holds, even if no boiler was fitted. This hinged access panel was later replaced with a fixed cover which was usually bolted in

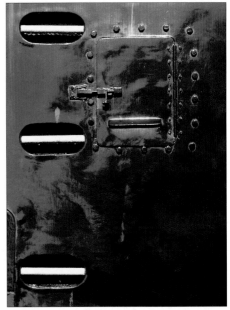

place and many locomotives also had the hand holds, which gave access to the water filler (in both positions), covered in with metal plates.

## Cab swaps and headcode box changes

The original locomotives were fitted with headcode discs but subsequently, with the adoption of headcode displays, locomotives from No D5114 were fitted with headcode boxes. However, the air horns were still fitted behind the buffer beam so the sides of the indicator boxes were flat. From No D5176 the indicator boxes also incorporated the air horns on either side and the sides of the box now sloped into the roof. The indicator boxes were integral with the cab. so when locomotives were observed with different ones this was as a result of a cab swap. as the box could not be removed separately from the cab.

A number of locomotives received a modified headcode box, however, where it

was the same shape as the type incorporating the air horns, but with the air horn casings missing. This was presumably replacing either accident damage or corrosion as these replacement headcode boxes were sometimes fitted to only one end and this applied only to locomotives in the number range D5114 to D5175. These were originally fitted with headcode boxes which did not incorporate the air horns, so

Class 24/0 No 24049 (D5049) (Crewe 4/1960) is dumped on the scrap line at Swindon Works displaying a very unusual modification in that despite being built without any headcode boxes, it has acquired one from a Class 24/1 at one end while retaining its disc headcodes.
The only other known example of this fitment was No 24055.

**Class 24/1 No 5148 (24148) (Derby 12/1960), at Sheffield Midland on 20 June 1970, shows the non-standard headcode boxes which have 'wings', but without the shrouds for the air horn. Whilst some locomotives received these at one end only, this example has them on both ends. It displays the first version of the blue livery with double arrows at both ends and the number carried twice on each side.** *N. E. Preedy*

presumably the horns were retained in their original position behind the buffer beam. Examples include No D5147 (24147) seen in 1968 when still in green and with modified headcode boxes fitted at both ends. This retained these modified boxes in 1971 when in blue, but was still numbered 5147. Also, No 5148 (seen in June 1970 in blue livery).

The same batch of locomotives (Nos D5114 to D 5176) was also occasionally fitted with the last style of headcode box incorporating the air horn receptacles. Examples known to have been so equipped included Nos 24134, 24142, 24147 (in green with full yellow ends), 25006, 25008, 25010 and 25015.

Some locomotives were fitted with two different modified headcode boxes, so Nos 24134 and 25006 had a winged box at one end and one with air horn shrouds at the other.

In June 1976, the use of train reporting numbers was abandoned and initially the headcode blinds displayed '0000', and then a blank blind with two white circles (known as dominoes).

The strangest modification was made to Nos 24049 and 24055 in that having been built without headcode boxes, both acquired a '24/1' box at one end while retaining the indicator discs at the end with the indicator box. This feature was certainly retained by No 24049 until it was scrapped at Swindon in 1976.

Class 24/1 No 24147 (D5147) (Derby 12/1960) was one of the Class 24/1s fitted with non-standard headcode boxes with winged side extensions, similar to those on the later Class 25/1s, but without the air-horn covers. Unusually, in this case the modified headcode boxes have been fitted to both ends. *B. J. Nicolle*

## Consett iron ore modification

In the mid-1960s, a number of Class 24s replaced the '9F' class 2-10-0s on the Consett iron ore trains on the line between Tyne Dock and Consett steel works, which had some severe gradients, and they were used in pairs. To work the air-operated hopper doors on the iron ore wagons, the locomotives were therefore fitted with a high-level air pipe (which looked like a steam-era vac pipe), fed by an additional air compressor. Locomotives allocated to Gateshead were Nos D5096 to D5113 (24102 to 24111) and from these Nos D5102 to D5111 were selected for the Consett workings. They had their train-heat boilers and water tanks removed as the additional compressor occupied the space where the boiler used to be. When this service ceased with the closure of Consett Iron Works in the 1970s, the locomotives were reallocated to other depots, but many retained the additional air pipe, some until they were withdrawn.

Class 24/0 No D5006 (24006) (Derby 1/1959) is at Ashford on 19 July 1959 when on loan to the Southern Region due to the late delivery of the BRCW Type 3s. Following concerns by the SR Civil Engineer regarding the weight of the locomotives, the steam-heat boiler water tank was temporarily removed, as seen here. The split radiator grille and the two-rung steps are indicators of the first batch of locomotives built. *P. H. Groom*

## Steam-heating water tank removal

Many of the class were never fitted with steam-heat boilers and therefore were not fitted with the associated water tank, while a number of locomotives which had a water tank fitted originally, later had this removed. Examples include Nos 24034, 24035, 24039, 24063 (1975) and 24134, as well as Nos D5102 to D5111, the Consett locomotives.

Only one Class 25 originally fitted with a steam-heat boiler and water tank is known to have had its tank removed, this being No 25242.

As mentioned previously, the locomotives sent to the Southern Region in 1959 had the water tanks removed temporarily, for example, No D5006, but these were subsequently reinstated.

Class 24/0
No 24035 (D5035)
(Crewe 8/1959).
The locomotive was
originally fitted with
steam-heat water
tanks, but by the
time this photograph
was taken at
Stourbridge Junction
in June 1978 the
water tank had been
removed. The works
plate has been moved
to the door, and the
hand holds on the
bodyside to access
the water filler hatch
have been plated
over. *G. W. Sharpe*

Class 24/1 24063 (D5063) (Crewe 1/1960) at Gloucester Horton Road depot on
25 June 1975 has had its steam-heat boiler water tank removed. The locomotive
also has the nose doors welded up and has the later-style sandboxes fitted.
The hand holds to access the water filler have also been plated over, as has
one of the ventilation grilles over the cab door. *N. E. Preedy*

## Air brakes

The class was originally fitted with vacuum brakes, but as air-braked stock became more common it was clear that the Sulzer Type 2s should also be fitted, so from No D7568 (25218) onwards, most new locomotives were additionally fitted with air-brake equipment (which required an extra compressor), as were a number of earlier Class 25s subsequently. No Class 24s were air-brake fitted, but a total of 110 Class 25s received dual brakes between 1973 and 1979. The air-braking capability could be identified by the additional hoses in the buffer beams and the Class 25s with the early body style, by hinges on the grilles on the bodyside. These grilles were necessary as the additional equipment in the already cramped body blocked access to the filters from the inside, thus requiring external access. Examples of '25s' with the original body style which were retrofitted included Nos 25028, 25033, 25034, 25035 and 25059.

## Snowplough fitment

A number of the Scottish-based examples of the '24/1' and old-style body '25s' were fitted with snowploughs. Some London Midland Region-based locomotives were also fitted with snowploughs, although these were usually the revised body style Class 25/2 and 25/3s. These included transfers from the Scottish Region and therefore had the ploughs already fitted when they arrived at their new depots. It

Class 25/3 No 7669 (25319) (Derby 3/1967) pauses at Guide Bridge on 21 March 1973 in the early form of blue livery and is fitted with snowploughs. These were normally associated with the Scottish Region, but with locomotive transfers they could also be seen on the LM Region. The sandboxes are of the early type and no steam-heat boiler water tank is fitted. *NEP*

51

Snowplough fitment to the '24/1s' and '25s' seems to have been common, but such items on '24/0s' were less common, especially away from the north of England. However, No D5077 (24077) (Crewe 2/1960) was observed at Barmouth on the Cambrian main line sporting a snowplough in the late 1960s.
*John Conway*

was unusual for the early Class 24s on the LM Region to have such fittings, but certainly No D5077 was seen with these in place at Barmouth in the 1960s.

Other examples seen are as follows: No 5176 (at Holyhead), 25027 (1976) Wigan Springs Branch, 25035 (1981) Stoke (Cockshute), 25036 (1978) Wigan Springs Branch, 25039 (1980) Longsight, 25043 (1976) Liverpool (Speke Junction), 25044 (1984) Cricklewood, 25191 (1978) Altrincham, 25224 (1980 and '82) Crewe, Helsby and (1983) Tyseley.

The fitting of snowploughs was dependent on having the correct brackets installed under the locomotive.

Class 25 No D5209 (25059) (Derby, 7/1963) is seen fitted with snowploughs in January 1987. The nose doors have been welded up and the blue stars are located inboard of the buffers. The livery displays evidence of a Glasgow repair so is likely to have been a Scottish-based locomotive. *Robert C. Jones*

## Polished grille surrounds

Some of the Darlington-built locomotives had the grille surrounds in polished aluminium rather than being painted when they were delivered. These were presumably painted over at the first visit to a works.

## Works and builder's plates

These were cast in aluminium and, for the locomotives built by the BR workshops, were originally fixed below the cab window in front of the door. When repainted into blue livery many had the works plates moved to the cab door as the original position was where the double arrow was applied. The batch built at Beyer Peacock, Nos D7624 to D7659 (25274 to 25309) was delivered with the builder's plates affixed to the cab doors.

The works plates fitted to No D5000 were unique as they incorporated the BR emblem on either side of the building details.

The works plates for No D5000 (No 24005) (Derby 8/1958) were different from all those on locomotives built subsequently as they had the BR emblem featured twice on each plate. *BR*

The works plate fitted to No D5032, built at Crewe. The plates were usually painted black.

Class 25/2 No D5223 (25073) (Darlington 7/1963) is admired at Cricklewood open day in 1969. The works plate has been moved to the door, being displaced from its original position by the double arrows under the cab windows. Visible are the revised bodyside air intakes which have a less prominent surround than previously fitted. The two holes at the bottom of both doors are for retaining them open and mate with two extensions under the lamp brackets. *G. W. Sharpe*

No 25053 (Derby 6/1963, ex 5203) with No 25235 behind are seen on a cement train at Wrexham on 25 April 1975. The hole in the middle of the nose just above the bufferbeam was an access hole for a communication cable when working the Royal Trains.
*David Cousins*

## Royal Train Blanking Plates/Access Holes

A small blanking plate (approx 2in diameter) was fitted to a number of locomotives used on Royal Train duties. The blanking plates (fitted on the lower portion of the nose) allowed a cable to be strung from the front cab back into the train to allow the travelling inspector to talk to the Royal Train staff. This fitment seems to have been confined to Class 24s and the original body style 25s. Examples include Nos 24136, 25052 and 25053.  This must not be confused with the two holes at the bottom of the nose doors. Examples include Nos 24062, 24082, 5056, 25043, 5165, D5038, D5165 and 5176 , which were used to keep the nose door open by mating with two extensions underneath the lamp bracket.

## Cab ventilation grilles

As built, Classes 24/0, 24/1, 25/0 and 25/1 were all fitted with a small square grille above the four cab doors, but many locomotives subsequently had one or more plated over, so for example, No 24063 in 1974 had ventilators at one end, but not the other.

## BR green

No D5000 had a livery unique to the class. It was out-shopped from Derby in the standard BR locomotive green with a single stripe in eggshell colour around the body at waist level. The D5000 number was placed a little lower on the cab side, level with the bottom of the radiator grille. This one-off livery was retained until 1969 when it was repainted in blue.

Subsequently, the rest of the class were painted green with a pale blue stripe at the bottom of the sill and another at the join between the body and the roof. The stripe at the top of the body was not always replaced when the locomotives visited works (for example, No D5133 observed in 1969). When delivered, the vertical cab hand rails were painted white, but many locomotives were seen with these painted green, or in a natural steel finish. When, from No D5176 (25026), the valance was removed, the pale blue stripe along the bottom of the bodyside was painted a couple of inches higher, which resulted in it no longer being at the bottom of the cab side. Locomotives completed at Derby Works were brush

*Class 25/2 No D5226 (25076) (Darlington 8/1963) shunts at Claydale sidings, Harpenden, on a local working on 17 August 1965. The yellow warning panel (with rounded corners) on the nose has not been painted over the lower body stripe, unlike on many other examples. Only one overhead warning flash has been fitted to the nose.* G. W. Sharpe

Two green '24s' were observed with the BR double-arrow symbol instead of the standard totem. No D5113 (24113) (Darlington 1/1961) was one, as seen here with No 24082 (D5082) (Crewe 7/1960) on the scrap line at Swindon in 1976. The blue data panel can be clearly seen against the faded green livery.

painted as there was no extraction equipment in the paint shop.

Locomotives built at Darlington (such as Nos D5151 to D5175) had the bodyside grilles painted grey and sometimes the grille surrounds were polished. Snowploughs, when fitted, were painted either green or black.

In the transitional period between the green livery and blue, a number of locomotives were seen with green bodysides but without the pale blue line at the bottom, presumably as a result of depot patch painting.

A number of locomotives retained their green livery when renumbered into the TOPS 24xxx and 25xxx series, including Nos 24044, 24063, 24082, 24057, 24090 (1975), 24092 (1975), 24136 (1975), 25036, 25038, and 25043 (still with a lower body stripe in

1976). By this date, the locomotives were usually in plain green without the lower body stripe. A number of other locomotives were reported in green with TOPS numbers, including Nos 24032, 24035, 24039, 24047, 24069, 24071, 24081, 24110 25006, 25040, 25053, 25058, 25102, 25202, 25203, 25218, 25248, 25251, 25252, 25260, 25261, 25278, 25279, 25285, 25294 and 25305 but have not been verified by the author.

A few Class 24s and 25s reached 1975 still sporting a very faded green livery with full yellow ends (Nos 24090, 25043 and two-tone green, 25102 and 25294). Nos 25043 and 25102 were the last locomotives to be repainted from green to blue, when they received overhauls in April 1976 at Derby.

A couple of green '24s' had an unusual livery variation. No D5113 was seen in 1968 sporting its original livery (with small yellow warning panel), but with just one double arrow in the middle of the bodyside. No 24092 was noted at Swindon in 1976 awaiting scrapping, in green (with full yellow ends), also with a double-arrow symbol.

Class 25/2 No D7549 (25199) (Derby 5/1965) is in as-built condition with small yellow warning panel (with square corners). *Class Twenty Locomotive Society*

Class 24/0 No D5038 (24038) (Crewe 9/1959) is seen at Crewe in 1971 still sporting its two-tone green livery which it acquired in 1965, but with the addition of a full yellow end and a blue data panel in front of the works plate. The valances are still fitted as are the original-style fuel and water tanks (although the fuel tank has acquired a gauge).

## BR two-tone green

This livery appeared on the first of the new body style Class 25/2s built at Derby in December 1963 and became the standard livery for all the new body style Class 25/2s and 25/3s. The '25/2s' built to the older body style at the same time as the two-tone green examples retained the original livery (plain green with grey/blue band around the bottom of the body).

In 1965, Derby Works out-shopped a small number of Class 24s in the two-tone green livery, these being Nos D5005, D5037, D5038, D5040 and D5053. This was still carried by No D5053 in 1971 (complete with small yellow warning panel) and No D5038 with full yellow ends, also in 1971. As with the plain green examples, a number of two-tone green locomotives had full yellow ends when renumbered in the 25xxx series, including Nos 25248, 25279 (1974) and 25294.

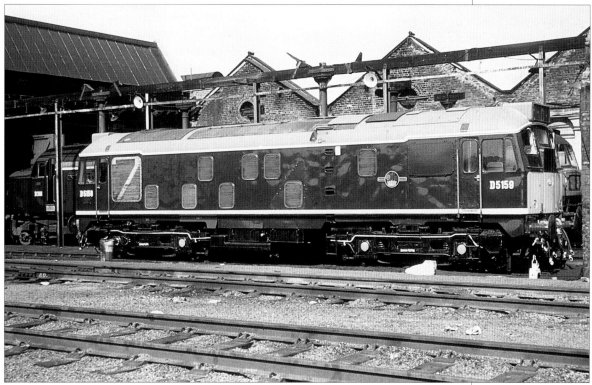

Class 25/0 No D5159
(25009) (Darlington
7/1961) is seen at
Haymarket shed,
Edinburgh, in May
1966 in what
appears to be
ex-works livery.
The yellow warning
panel goes to the
bottom of the nose,
covering the body
stripe.
This locomotive
was never fitted with
a steam-heat boiler
and therefore was
not fitted with a
water tank.
*Class Twenty
Locomotive Society*

**Top left:**
Class 24/0 No D5036 (24036) (Crewe 9/1959) is in original condition with the addition of a small yellow warning panel with rounded corners, which covers the lower body stripe. The headcode discs are edged in black and a patch on the nose shows where a shedplate had been fitted. The train reporting number (in the absence of a headcode box) has been stuck in the middle windscreen. *Colour-Rail*

**Left:**
Class 25/2 No D5214 (25064) (Derby 7/1963) was on Bedford shed in March 1970. The yellow warning panel has been painted over the lower body stripe on the nose, and three overhead warning flashes are fitted on the front. It has the later-style sandboxes, and the hand holds to access the boiler water filler have been plated over. A blue data panel has been applied to the far (No 1) end. *G. W. Sharpe*

## Yellow warning panels

### Small

A small yellow warning panel began to appear from 1962, the first version generally having rounded corners, but from about 1965 the corners became square, although this may have been due to regional variations. There was considerable variation in the application of this warning panel; some had the panel stopping at the bottom of the nose (covering the body stripe) and some finished at the body stripe, while on others the top of the panel came up level with the horizontal hand rails. A small number were also observed with the bottom corners of the panel also rounded. Examples include No D5114.

Because the two classes were built over a number of years, locomotives constructed from late 1962 were delivered new, with small yellow warning panels, such as Nos D5186 to D5222 at Derby in 1963.

Class 24/1 No 5095 (24095) (Darlington 3/1960) is seen at Edinburgh Haymarket in green livery with full yellow ends and a blue-backed data panel under the number. *ExeRail*

### Large

A large yellow warning panel covering the whole front started to be applied from 1967 and a number of green-painted locomotives received this feature, examples including Nos 5082 (1973) and after renumbering to 24082, 5142 (1972), 5147 (1971), 7574 (1972), D7595 and D7597. There were small variations in the application, with some having the front valances and the sides of the buffer beam also yellow, but with the central part of the buffer beam remaining red.

Class 24/2 No 5142 (24142 and TDB968009) (Derby 11/1960) passes Crewe on 20 July 1972 with a freight, showing the application of a full yellow end to a green-painted locomotive before renumbering in the TOPS 24xxx series. Both fuel and water tanks have reduced capacity and the centre section of the valance has been removed. The second wagon in the train was built specifically for carrying sheet glass from St Helens. *John Phillips*

Class 24/1 No D5078 (24078) (Crewe 2/1960) at Derby on 17 March 1968, in the first version of the blue livery. This had two small double arrows under the cab windows and the 'D' number repeated on each body side. The works plate has been relocated to the cab door. The hand rails are painted white and the sandboxes have been changed to the later type. Both fuel and water tanks have been reduced in capacity, with gauges fitted to both The full yellow warning panel also included the area around the bufferbeams.
*D. L. Percival*

## Rail blue

The first Class 24 to be repainted in BR blue was No D5068 which received its new livery in December 1966. The whole locomotive was painted blue including the roof, and it had a full yellow end. As with the green-painted locomotives, many had the vertical cab hand rails painted white, but it was not unusual to see these hand rails in blue or left in a natural steel finish. Where a snowplough was fitted it was generally painted yellow.

The majority of the class which had the first version of the blue livery had the large BR double arrows at each end under the cab windows with the locomotive number placed twice on the bodyside (adjacent to the cab doors), initially with a 'D' prefix and then subsequently without.

The livery was later simplified with just one small double arrow in the middle of the bodyside and the numbers were then moved back to the cab side, under the window, initially with the numbers at both ends. This revised scheme was implemented as the class was being renumbered, so many examples could be seen with the small arrow on the bodyside, but with its original number, with or without the 'D' prefix.

When 24xxx numbers were introduced and coupled with the one double arrow, it was normally applied to one end only under the driver's window, with the other cab side blank.

The major blue livery variant was that of locomotives painted at St Rollox Works in Glasgow where the single number was placed on the bodyside inboard of the cab side and not under the window, again with the data panel under the number. With this variant, the number sizes also varied, Glasgow using larger figures than other works.

At least two locomotives were repainted in blue livery but retained the BR lion-and-wheel totem (or 'ferret and dartboard' as it was known to enthusiasts), these being Nos 5021 (and retaining the totem when renumbered 24021) and 24090, the latter also having a grey roof.

The last 18 locomotives (Nos D7660 to D7677) out-shopped from Derby Works were delivered in the new corporate blue livery, the first two (Nos D7660 and D7661) with small yellow warning panels and the remainder with full yellow ends. These locomotives had double arrows at both ends and two Dxxxx numbers on both sides, inboard of the cab doors.

Some unusual and non-standard livery variations were noted, including one where the 'D' number was under the cab window

Class 24/1 No D5146 (24146) (Derby 12/1960) is in the first version of blue livery as applied from late 1966, with two sets of small double arrows and the 'D' number repeated on both sides. The cab hand rails are white, and both fuel and water tanks have reduced capacity and are fitted with gauges. *S. V. Blencowe*

Class 25/2 No 25226 (D7576) (Derby 11/1963) displays the Glasgow Works interpretation of blue livery at Perth in April 1982, with larger numbers and the blue stars located inboard on the nose. The locomotive has been fitted with air brakes and hinges to the small bodyside grilles. *Class Twenty Locomotive Society*

and the double arrows were on the cab doors, but unfortunately it has not been possible to identify the locomotive concerned. Another variation was double arrows under both cab windows, with the two sets of numbers on the bodyside and, additionally, smaller double arrows on both cab doors (giving a total of four double arrows per side) which was observed on No 5150 in 1973. No 25222 was also observed with both the number and double arrow under the driver's window.

Class 25/2 No 25241 (D7591) (Darlington 6/1964) is in the Glasgow-style livery with the number on the bodyside and data panel underneath with the shedcode below that. The blue stars on the nose are located closer to the centre than those applied by other regions. The nose doors have been plated over and the valance removed. *Author's collection*

**Class 24/1 No 24090 (D5090) (Crewe, 6/1960) Only two Class 24s are known to have carried blue livery but with the BR 'lion and wheel' emblem, and No 24090 is seen stored sporting this livery, but unusually also with a grey roof. The valances have been removed and the fuel and water tanks modified.** *Rail Image Collections*

Class 24/0 No 5021 (24021) (Derby 8/1959) was one of two Class 24s to receive blue livery but retaining the BR lion-and-wheel emblem, rather than being given double-arrow symbols. The cab hand rails are painted white and the valances have been removed. Although the locomotive, here resting at Crewe Diesel Depot, is boiler-fitted, the hand holds to access the water filler have been plated over, indicating the boiler is probably no longer in use. The boiler water tank has been shortened.
*Class Twenty Locomotive Society*

## Yellow warning panels

### Small

At the time the Rail blue livery was first applied, full yellow ends were already in use. However, as well as the two locomotives mentioned above (Nos D7660 and D7661) which were delivered new in blue with small yellow warning panels, at least three other members of the class received small yellow warning panels while in blue livery, namely Nos D5213 (with double arrow symbol), D5218 and D5226, both with BR lion-and-wheel totems. Nos D5213 and D5218 had both been repaired at Brush in Loughborough and there was some confusion at the private works as to how to repaint them, hence the small yellow warning panels.

### Large

This was applied from 1966 and became the standard feature for blue locomotives and also appeared on a number retaining green livery.

## Experimental warning panels

During 1966, two of Thornaby's Type 2s were trialled with fluorescent front warning panel, No D5159 being seen with a red front panel on 12 September 1966. This experiment appears to have been short-lived and how long this was used is not known to the author.

## Departmental livery

No 24061 became a departmental loco-motive in 1975 receiving the number RDB968007, retaining its original blue livery but with its number in small letters below the cab window (at one end on each side). In 1979, it passed to the Railway Technical Centre, Derby, and was renumbered 97201 and acquired a new livery with a broad red band along the top two-thirds of the bodyside, edged with white. The lower bodyside remained in blue. The double arrow was placed further along the bodyside to be in the centre of the red panel and it later carried the painted name *Experiment*.

No D5061 (24061) (Crewe 1/1960) is seen at Nottingham on 15 November 1979 as No 97201, displaying its Railway Technical Centre, Derby, red and blue livery. It had previously been in Departmental stock as No RDB968007 (11/1975–8/1979). Later-style sandboxes have been fitted and the valances have been removed. The name *Experiment* was applied to this locomotive in July 1980. The livery is the same as the specialised coaching stock. The locomotive was subsequently preserved and can be seen today on the North Yorkshire Railway back in its original green livery. *G. Grafton*

Class 24/1 No D5149
(Derby 1/1961) runs
round at Tyne
Commission Quay
on 30 July 1966.
It has a small yellow
warning panel and a
shedplate on the nose.
This locomotive
was withdrawn in
October 1973 having
been badly damaged
and so never carried
its 24xxx series
number. *G. W. Sharpe*

## Renumbering

When the decision was made in 1973 to
renumber all diesel and electric locomotives
with the class prefix under the TOPS
classification, the Sulzer Type 2s became
Classes 24 and 25. For the Class 24
locomotives this followed the format of
dropping the leading '5' and putting the
class number in front, so No D5001 became
24001. As the TOPS computer (Total
Operations Processing System) could not
recognise '000' figures (for D5000) and as
No D5005 had already been withdrawn
through accident damage, No D5000
became 24005.

For the Class 25s, renumbering was more
complex as the original 'D' numbers
continued on from the Class 24s, but their
numbers needed to start at 25001, even
though the first locomotive was No D5151,
so only the last digit was carried over. The
class was therefore renumbered as follows:

D5000 = 24005 (Class 24/0)
D5001 to D5049 = 24001 to 24049
  (Class 24/0)
D5050 to D5150 = 24050 to 24150
  (Class 24/1)
D5151 to D5175 = 25001 to 25025
  (Class 25/0)
D5176 to D5232 = 25026 to 25082
  (Class 25/1)
D5233 to D5299 = 25083 to 25149
  (Class 25/2)
D7500 to D7567 = 25150 to 25217
  (Class 25/3)
D7568 to D7597 = 25218 to 25247
  (Class 25/2)
D7598 to D7677 = 25248 to 25327
  (Class 25/3)

Several locomotives had been withdrawn
before being renumbered, including No
D5005 (its 24005 number used for D5000),
but for the others, gaps were left in the
24xxx and 25xxx sequence so No 24028, for

example, was not used for the previously withdrawn No D5028. Likewise, those which were withdrawn prior to the use of TOPS numbers were Nos D5043 (24043), D5051 (24051), D5067 (24067), D5068 (24068), D5088 (24088), D5093 (24093), D5114 (24114), D5122 (24122), D5131 (24131), D5138 (24138), D5139 (24139), D5149 (24149), D5278 (25218) and D7605 (25265).

During 1986, a small number of the class were renumbered into a new sub class '25/9' as part of a sectorisation idea, these being Nos 25901 to 25912. The renumbered locomotives were previously Nos 25262, 25268, 25276, 25283, 25286, 25296, 25297, 25307, 25309, 25315, 25316 and 25322 respectively.

## Data panels

With the decision to renumber locomotives into the TOPS scheme, a data panel was placed on the bodyside giving details of the class type, speed, weight, etc. This was a transfer with a blue background, so when placed on a green-painted locomotive it stood out. The general rule seems to have been that the panel should be adjacent to the number, so that when the driver booked on to a locomotive and when checking the number, he would be able to see the data panel easily.

With the first version of the blue livery double arrows were applied on both ends and the numbers placed on the bodyside with the data panel underneath it. When the livery was simplified to one double arrow in the middle of the bodyside, the data panel was able to be moved to the cab side with the number.

The position of the data panel varied, particularly when the works plate was still fixed to the bodyside under the cab window, forcing the data panel to be placed above or below this plate, but sometimes in front of it. With the removal of the works plates or their repositioning to the cab doors, the data panel tended to be placed under the cab side window, in the centre.

**Two Class 25/3s, Nos D7558 (25208) (Derby 9/1965) and D7550 (25200) (Derby 6/1965), stabled nose to nose, both in green with full yellow ends, but with No D7550 having a blue data panel and snowploughs.**
*Author's collection*

Class 24/0 No 24009 (D5009) (Derby, 3/1958) at Glasgow Eastfield in 1975 showing the 'Glasgow' style of painting with the number on the bodyside and the data panel below. The doors have been welded up and the headcode discs centred in the door. The blue stars have been located closer to the nose door.
*N. E. Preedy*

## Numbers on the nose

A selection of locomotives had their number painted on the nose (usually by shed staff). Examples included Nos 25048 on the Western Region with white-painted figures applied at the bottom of the nose front, and 25081 (1979) which was observed with the additional numbers in black on the nose doors, just below the level of the nose hand rails. No 25035 had the numbers in the black near the bottom of the nose.

Class 25/1 No 25057 (D5207) (Derby 6/1963) passes Stafford on 24 February 1987, displaying its number on the nose. This is likely to have been applied at its home depot. The nose doors have been plated over and no blue stars are visible on the front. At this date, the remaining members of the class had only a few weeks of active service left.
*Chris Morrison*

## Shedcode plates and names

When the Class 24s were introduced many were fitted with steam-era cast-iron shedplates, as at that time the locomotives were allocated to steam depots, such as No D5000 to 5B, Crewe South. When fitted, oval shedcode plates were usually on the cab side, under the works plates (examples being Nos D5034 and D5076).

A number of locomotives allocated to the Eastern Region had the shedplate mounted on the nose of the locomotive, for example, Nos D5038, D5058, D5061, D5064 and D5087 of 51L, Thornaby, and 60A, Inverness, also followed this practice, examples including Nos 5126 and D5129.

With the repainting into blue livery and the adoption of TOPS, depots then used a two-letter abbreviated form of the shed name on a small blue transfer, usually edged with white. Examples include CF (Cardiff Canton), LO (Longsight, Manchester), ED (Eastfield, Glasgow) while, for a time, Inverness painted its name in small letters under the number on the cab side.

Class 25/0 No D5152 (25002) (Darlington 5/1961) in as-delivered condition, without a small yellow warning panel, displays a steam-style cast-iron shedplate on the nose door.
*Author's collection*

No D5076 (24076) (Crewe 02/1960) is on Willesden shed in 1964, displaying its 1A shedplate under the works plate.
*British Railways*

Class 24/1 No 5130 (24130) (Derby 9/60) rests between turns at Inverness. It is fitted with twin headlamps and tablet catchers as well as snowploughs. The valances have been removed and one of the modified boiler air-intake panels with five slots has been fitted. A shedplate is carried above the headlamps and the two blue stars are placed inboard of the nose corners, a sign the locomotive has been overhauled at Glasgow Works. The fuel and water tanks have been modified with reduced capacity and the sandboxes are of the first type. The extension spigots on the underside of the lower lamp bracket can clearly be seen and these mated with the two holes at the bottom of the nose doors. The nose doors also display the strip steel initially used to reduce draughts from the doors.
*Class Twenty Locomotive Society*

## Multiple working blue star indicator

All the locomotives displayed the standard two blue stars on the nose front at the bottom of the nose corners. However, those out-shopped from Glasgow Works had the blue stars placed more towards the centre of the locomotive and above the multiple working connections.

## Tamworth Castle

In May 1984, No 25322 was repainted for an exhibition at Tamworth and was given full yellow cabs including the sides. The body sides were blue and the cab roof was grey, with the cab window surrounds painted black. The locomotive retained this livery for the remainder of its operational career including the period it was renumbered as 25912, until it was withdrawn in March 1987. It then passed to the Training department at Leeds Holbeck where it was used for apprentice training. It was subsequently reinstated for use on enthusiast specials, but it was then painted in two-tone green, although this livery had never been carried previously, as it was built and delivered in BR blue. It is now preserved on the Churnet Valley Railway.

**Class 25/3 No 25322 (D7672) (Derby 2/1967) is seen in a one-off livery with black window frames, double arrows and lamp brackets and carrying the name** *Tamworth Castle*. **Despite being a late-built locomotive it has early-style sandboxes.**
*Colour-Rail*

Previous page:
Class 24/1,
No 97201 (24061
and D5061) (Crewe
1/1960) in Derby
research livery,
which it acquired
late in its life. The
fuel tank has been
modified and
original-style
sandboxes are fitted,
along with the nose
doors. *G. W. Sharpe*

## Departmental stock

Three Class 24s were transferred to Departmental stock, No D5061 becoming RDB968007 (11/1975 to 8/1979) and then 97201 (8/1979 to 1/1988) on becoming part of the Research Department at Derby, where named *Experiment* in July 1980.

Nos D5054 (24054) and D5142 (24142) were renumbered TDB968008 and TDB968009 respectively in August 1976, for use as train-heating generators. These two locomotives retained their blue livery but were renumbered with small lettering at one end. They were permanently connected to electrical connectors and did not move, two notices being affixed on either side giving instructions as to what to do in the event of a fire.

**Class 24/1 No ADB968008 (D5054 and 24054) (Crewe 12/1959) stands at Newton Abbot on 29 October 1981 where it had been adapted to provide train pre-heating. The fuel and water tanks have been modified and fitted with gauges, and revised-style sandboxes are fitted at one end. The hand holds on the bodyside have been plated over, as have the nose doors. Note the light attached to the cab roof (near the radiator air intake and the electrical cables under the front of the locomotive.**
*A. O. Wynn*

When the bulk of the class had been withdrawn, three were converted to train-heating units for use on the Glasgow–Fort William line where the newly introduced Mk3 sleeping cars had only electric train heating and the locomotives hauling the train were not so equipped. These were Nos 25310, 25305 and 25314 which were given Departmental numbers ADB97250 to ADB97252 and named *ETHEL 1* to *ETHEL 3* respectively. (ETHEL = Electric Train-Heating Ex-Locomotive.)

The traction motors were isolated, making it impossible for them to move under their own power. The livery was dark blue with a very pale blue panel for the top third of the bodyside with the ETHEL name stencilled on the bodyside on the pale blue section. The

**Departmental Unit No ADB 97250 ETHEL 1 is seen at Glasgow Eastfield depot in August 1983. The sandboxes have been removed from the bogies.**
*A. O. Wynn*

Departmental Unit No ADB 97252 ETHEL 3. Displaying the different styles of the light blue at each end. ETHEL 2 also had this style.
*Transport Images/ D. J. Clarke Collection*

No 97252 (25314, D7664) (Derby 11/1966) is repainted in InterCity livery. ETHEL 3 was used to provide heating for steam specials out of Marylebone which used electrically heated coaches.
*W. A. Sharman*

Highland line emblem of a 'Scottie dog' (actually a West Highland White terrier) was applied on a red background on the light blue part of the body as was the name, on a panel edged in red. There was a difference with the original livery applied to *ETHEL 2* and *3* which had the light blue panel sloping down at the ends with more of the cab side in the light blue.

When electric train-heat-fitted Class 37/4s became available to work the trains the units were made redundant from this service, except for occasional static train-heating. At the end of 1986, *ETHEL 3* was moved down to London Marylebone where it was used to provide heating for steam specials, such as the 'Shakespeare Expresses' between Marylebone and Stratford upon Avon, and becoming notoriously unpopular with photographers in the process! In an attempt to disguise it with the coaching stock it was repainted in early 1987 in InterCity livery (dark/light grey/black/red) with its *ETHEL 3* name placed below both cab sides. Nos ADB97251 and ADB97252 were also both repainted into InterCity livery.

**Class 25/0 No D5160 (25010) (Darlington 8/1961) heads a train of empty bolsters and plate wagons north of York. It has a 51L, Thornaby, shedplate on the nose and still has the original circular exhaust port. This batch of locomotives, Nos D5151 to D5175, was built without steam heating and therefore did not have water tanks.**
*J. B. Sugden*

## Allocations

Following running-in on local services around Derby, the first locomotives were initially allocated to Crewe South (5B). However, their stay was short-lived as in January 1959 the first seven locomotives were reallocated to Hither Green (73C) on the Southern Region. This was to cover workings in the London and Kent areas as the arrival of the BRCW Type 3s (later Class 33) had been delayed. A further batch, Nos D5007 to D5014, was soon after also allocated to Hither Green. These loco-motives remained on the Southern Region until 1962 when they moved back to the London Midland Region.

The next batch built was sent to Willesden (1A) and Camden (1B) for local passenger workings out of Euston, and another batch was sent to Finsbury Park on the Eastern Region for suburban workings out of King's Cross.

The pattern that emerges is of batches of locomotives sent to specific depots in sufficient numbers to allow certain services to be dieselised. So, for example, Nos D5096 to D5113 went to Gateshead for general duties (passenger, parcels and freight) and for the complete replacement of the '9F'

Class 24/1 No D5102 (24102) (Darlington 7/1960) is seen in Tyne Dock yard in September 1969 double-heading a Consett iron ore train with another member of the class and has the first blue livery and a faded yellow warning panel. There is an additional air hose above the buffer beam and the cab hand rails are painted white.
*G. W. Sharpe*

2-10-0 steam locomotives on the Consett iron ore trains. Similarly, 19 of the class were allocated to Inverness (60A) to allow complete dieselisation of the Highland main line (along with some BRCW Type 2s).

Nos D5151 to D5175, built in 1961 at Darlington, were all delivered to Thornaby to assist in the removal of local steam working in the Middlesbrough area. As this was essentially freight working these were built without steam-heat boiler and water tank. As with many other things, even though the batch was built without train-heat boiler, the boiler vent grille was still included as were the steps up the bodyside to the non-existent water tank filler!

A large number of newly built Class 25s were allocated to Toton (midway between Nottingham and Derby) for dieselisation of the Midland main line freight workings. Further members of the class were reallocated to this depot so that by the mid-1970s around 50 examples were allocated there.

As time passed, the class was allocated to Bescot (Walsall), Crewe, Springs Branch (Wigan), Longsight (Manchester), Allerton (Liverpool), Barrow, Leicester, Derby, Saltley (Birmingham), Tinsley (Sheffield), March (Cambridgeshire), Finsbury Park (North London), Wath (Sheffield), Neville Hill (Leeds), Inverness, Eastfield (Glasgow), and Haymarket (Edinburgh).

Class 25/3 No D7638 (25288) (Beyer Peacock 11/1965) powers an express passenger train through Mirfield on 22 June 1963 and shows the original circular exhaust and two-tone green livery with small yellow warning panel which it carried from new. This batch of 36 locomotives, Nos D7624 to D7659, was built under contract by Beyer Peacock of Gorton, none of which was fitted with steam-heat boilers and therefore did not have a water tank.
*G. W. Sharpe*

| Allocations Numbers in parentheses indicate Class 24 or 25 | | | |
|---|---|---|---|
| July 1962 (All Class 25) | March 1974 | June 1979 | October 1980 |
| 73C Hither Green 2 | Eastfield, Glasgow 30 (24), 11 (25) | Eastfield 40 (25) | Haymarket, Edinburgh 16 |
| 5A Crewe North 3 | Longsight, Manchester 7 (24), 30 (25) | Longsight 29 (25) | Crewe 31 |
| 1A Willesden 25 | Crewe 64 (24) | Crewe 1 (24), 46 (25) | Carlisle Kingmoor 18 |
| 1B Camden 7 | Haymarket, Edinburgh 14 (25) | Haymarket, Edinburgh 18 (25) | Longsight, 9 (24), Manchester 17 |
| 32B Ipswich 14 | Gateshead 9 (24) | Bescot 32 | Bescot 31 |
| 34G Finsbury Park 25 | Inverness 18 (24) | Inverness 3 (25) | Eastfield, Glasgow 23 |
| 14A Cricklewood, London 10 | Tinsley, Sheffield 28 (25) | | Cricklewood, London 42 |
| 52A Gateshead 26 | Ebbw Junction, Newport 12 (25) | | Toton 40 |
| 60A Inverness 19 | Cricklewood, London 14 (25) | Cricklewood, London 53 (25) | Springs Branch, Wigan 28 |
| 9A Longsight, Manchester 8 | Toton 52 (25) | Toton 43 (25) | |
| 51L Thornaby 30 | Carlisle Kingmoor 19 (25) | Carlisle Kingmoor 14 (25) | |
| 1C Watford 5 | Springs Branch, Wigan 50 (25) | Springs Branch, Wigan 22 (25) | |
| 2A Rugby 7 | Bath Road, Bristol 6 (25) | | |
| | Willesden, London 31 (25) | | |
| | Canton, Cardiff 12 (25) | | |
| | Laira, Plymouth 11 (25) | Laira, Plymouth 10 (25) | |

**Two Class 25s (Nos D5229, later 25079 and D7585, later 25235) pass through Tamworth on a loaded coal train in August 1967.** *Class Twenty Locomotive Society*

By the mid-1970s, around 50 members of the class were allocated to Springs Branch (Wigan) for freight working in the Manchester–Wigan–Liverpool area. A batch of locomotives was at one point allocated to Ebbw Junction, Newport, specifically for the iron ore trains between the docks and Ebbw Vale steel works, but the gradient and loading of the trains was beyond their power rating and these were soon replaced by the English Electric Type 3s (later Class 37).

In 1971, the class broke new ground when a number of '25s' were allocated to the Western Region to replace the unsuccessful Class 22 diesel-hydraulic Type 2s. The allocation went to Plymouth Laira and Bristol Bath Road and they could be seen on many of the Cornish branches on china clay trains as well as parcels traffic in the Bristol area. By 1980, the WR lost its allocation either by withdrawal or transfers back to the LM Region.

Class 25/1 No 5209 (No 25059) (Derby 6/1963) is stabled at Bristol Bath Road shed following transfer to the Western Region to replace the Class 22 diesel-hydraulics which had early withdrawal. It is in as-built condition but repainted blue with a shed name below the data panel. The hand holds for accessing the water filler have been plated over and a blanking plate covers the air intake for the steam-heat boiler. *Author's collection*

Two Class 24/2s, Nos 5127 (24127) (Derby 7/1960) in front and No 5121 (24121) (Derby 6/1960) leave Inverness with a 16-coach train to Glasgow and Edinburgh on 31 March 1974. No 5121 displays many modifications including the headcode box with wings, four slots in the boiler intake cover (instead of the more usual five) and welded-up nose doors. Both locomotives have tablet catchers, headlamps and snowploughs. *Brian Morrison*

Class 25/2 No 25227 (D7577) (Derby 11/1963) heads an up freight near Redruth on 9 July 1976. The Class 25s were a common site in Cornwall following their transfer to replace the withdrawn diesel-hydraulic Type 2s (Class 22) on mixed-traffic workings, particularly on china clay trains. The nose doors have been welded up and the revised bodyside air intakes with their less prominent surrounds can be seen. *Brian Morrison*

## Routes

Whilst the class could be seen over large portions of the network, they were particularly associated with specific routes and workings. For a long period through to the early 1980s, the Class 25s worked the Tunstead (Peak District) to Northwich (Cheshire) limestone trains, and the author well remembers the noise of a thrashed '25' as the trains came through Altrincham station.

From the mid-1970s, the boiler-fitted

Class 25s found themselves in the limelight as they were diagrammed to work the Crewe to Cardiff passenger services (with six BR Mk1 coaches) on a daily basis and continued on this duty until replaced by Class 33s in April 1981.

The Sulzer Type 2s will be long associated with both the Cambrian main line, where they had a virtual monopoly of both passenger and freight workings, and with the Highland main line, although in this instance they shared duties with the BRCW Type 2s.

In the last days of the Class 25s they were used regularly on summer Saturday trains including workings from the East Midlands to Skegness, Yarmouth, Llandudno, Blackpool and Scarborough. Many of these workings were double-headed and attracted a large number of enthusiasts to join the holidaymakers.

**Class 25/2
No D5277 (25127)
(Derby 6/1964)
passes Chinley with
empty hoppers from
Northwich to Peak
Forest on 31 March
1967. The Class 25s
were long associated
with this traffic.
The locomotive was
still fitted with a
circular exhaust port
at this time.**
*J. H. Cooper-Smith*

Top left:
Class 25/2 No 25219 (D7569) (Derby 10/1963) passes Gresty Lane No 1 signalbox, on the outskirts of Crewe, with the 12.20 Crewe–Cardiff service on 23 March 1979. This was one of a stud of steam-heat boiler-fitted locomotives retained for this service. *P. Kynaston*

Bottom left:
The Class 24s and 25s were used regularly on Royal Trains away from the main line and Nos 25221 (D7571) and 25222 (D7572) (both Derby 10/1963) head Royal Train empty stock on the Cambrian main line near Fairbourne on 22 June 1977. *Ian Allan Library*

Class 25/1 No 25058 (D5208) (Derby, 7/1963) at Stamford in May 1981 with a cement train. The headcode box now has the 'dominoes' displayed. The number is located very close to the cab window with the data panel underneath. The later style sandboxes are also fitted. *W. A. Sharman*

Top right:
Class 25/2 No D5243 (No 25093) (Derby 1/1964) is seen at Toton depot receiving maintenance on 22 February 1968. The ATC contact shoe can be clearly seen at the front of the bogie. The later style of sandbox is fitted, but it does not have a water tank or steam-heat equipment. The two bolt heads below the works plate indicate where a cast-iron shedplate has been fitted. *BR*

Lower right:
No 25322 (D7672), (25912) (Derby 2/1967) *Tamworth Castle* is seen in its unique livery with the cab sides painted yellow with black window surrounds and the double arrows also in black. *Brian Morrison*

## Foreign travels

Being at one time allocated to the London Midland, Western, Eastern, North Eastern and Scottish regions, there were not many places that did not see a Class 24/25 on a regular basis as they could be seen from Penzance to Wick. The only region not to have a long-term allocation was the Southern, although it had been allocated some for a short period, from 1959 to

## Repairs and repair locations

Having been built at BR Crewe, Derby and Darlington works and by Beyer Peacock, the class was maintained at various times at the following BR works: Glasgow (Cowlairs), Crewe, Darlington, Derby, Doncaster, Eastleigh, Glasgow (St Rollox), Inverurie, Stratford and Swindon, although Derby and Glasgow carried out most of the heavy overhauls. Locations such as Swindon generally undertook only unclassified repairs and many works visits were the result of accident damage.

In November and December 1965, a number of BR Sulzer Type 2s were repaired at the Brush works at Loughborough, the

## Withdrawals

The majority of early withdrawals were generally the result of accident damage, and subsequently by changes in traffic patterns; a sudden downturn in traffic could result in early examples being withdrawn. The lightweight construction of the body and cabs did not taking kindly to impacts such as with other locomotives. Also, there was a decline in general freight traffic, robbing the class of much of its original work, and then the cost of a major repair would lead to the withdrawal of the locomotive.

The electrification of the West Coast main line also reduced the requirement for Type 2

summer 1962. However, summer excursions to Brighton regularly saw these locomotives, usually double-headed.

The class never attracted the attention of enthusiasts as did the Class 40s, 50s, 52s and 55s, say, and therefore enthusiast workings away from their natural habitat were not common. Those enthusiast trains that did run tended to remain on their normal routes such as the use of No 25322 *Tamworth Castle* on the Settle and Carlisle line.

company having previously carried out work on behalf of BR by refurbishing a batch of 'Peaks'.

The modular design of the '24s' and '25s' led to the major components being interchangeable within the main sub groups. For example, during its main line operational life, the preserved No D7629 was fitted with six different engines, six main generators and five bogies.

Depots such as Toton (a purpose-built diesel facility) could undertake many repairs previously requiring a visit to a main works and needed to send away engines, generators and bogies only for specialised overhaul, with the stripping out of the components being done at the depot.

locomotives on the LM Region and the introduction of HSTs meant that more powerful diesel locomotives could be cascaded into freight service.

The withdrawal of the Class 24/25s started early with No D5051 in 1967 and No D5122 following an accident in September 1968. In July 1969, a freak accident at Chester resulted in a runaway iron ore train being switched into the diesel depot and colliding with five Class 24s, leading to the withdrawal of four of them (Nos D5043, D5093, D5138 and D5139). The first Class 25 withdrawn was No D5278 which went in 1971, the result of a runaway in the Peak Forest area in May of that year, and it was followed by

TAMWORTH CASTLE

No D7605 in March 1972. Subsequent withdrawals were often the result of the need for major (and costly) overhauls.

The increase of electrification and the reduction of wagon-load traffic all contributed to the decline in operating requirements for smaller Type 2 locomotives. Mass withdrawals of Class 24s started in 1975 and by 1976 only 12 remained, but the survivors lingered on until October 1980 when the last one was withdrawn from capital stock.

## Disposal

By the time that the class began to be disposed of, the policy of selling to private scrap merchants, prevalent at the end of steam, had changed and most were broken up at BR workshops. However, a number were sold to Vic Berry at Leicester (who also scrapped some examples at Thornton Junction shed in Scotland). The group of locomotives destroyed in the accident at Chester shed, when they were hit by a runaway iron ore train, were scrapped by Cashmores in the West Midlands.

Locomotives were often stored initially at depots and, in some cases, smaller service-able components were removed before they were sent to a works. Having arrived at one of the workshops, the larger components

The Class 25s then became the target and withdrawals continued at a steady rate during the late 1970s and early '80s until all had been withdrawn by 1987, the last operational survivor being No 25912 (previously 25322 and D7672), which was turned off on 23 March 1987. The locomotive, however, was reinstated at Leeds Holbeck shed and ran enthusiast specials on the Settle and Carlisle line between 1989 and 1991 until its second (and final) withdrawal.

including engines, traction motors, generators and compressors were sometimes removed before the locomotive was finally broken up. This was undertaken either at the receiving works or, as in many cases, it was forwarded to Swindon or Doncaster works for final scrapping, or the remains were sold on to one of the private contractors.

The removal of components resulted in many locomotives spending a considerable amount of time stored in a semi-derelict condition and. in some cases, being scrapped more than a year after being withdrawn from traffic. The works concerned with final disposals were Derby, Doncaster and Swindon. Even though Derby built the bulk of the Class 24s, the only one to be scrapped there was the collision-damaged No D5005 in 1969. Derby did, however, break up many of the '25s'.

## Summary

The Class 24s and 25s underwent numerous modifications as they were built over a period of nine years (from 1958 to 1967) and had two distinct body styles. They also incorporated features that, in some examples, were redundant from the outset, like the fitting of access steps to reach a steam-heat boiler filler when no such item was fitted.

BR certainly got their money's worth out of the class though, but by the 1980s they

were becoming worn out and suffering from major body corrosion which further increased their repair costs. There had always been issues with the traction motors and in the 1970s the number of failures had reached 200 in one year, with some locomotives requiring all four motors to be replaced.

Whilst generally reliable, the habit of the Operating Department to hang huge trains from the drawbar meant they were constantly being thrashed, with resultant dips in reliability.

The railway heritage movement has ensured that a good number of the Sulzer 2s have been preserved and there are examples across the country, although many are not operational and one or two are in very poor condition. The fact of having made it into preservation does not ensure a permanent life, as a number of other classes have had examples scrapped subsequently. It is to be hoped that this fate does not overtake any of the Class 24 and 25s. They are very popular with the permanent way departments of the heritage railways as they can haul any load and don't need five hours to raise steam. All the body styles are represented and many of the liveries have been reproduced, as well as some never actually carried by the class when in main line service.

Although Derby built the first of the Class 24s followed by many of the others, none of the preserved '24s' were built at that works, all four survivors being Crewe-built, and so no Darlington-built examples survive either. On the other hand, all three builders of the '25s' — Darlington, Derby and Beyer Peacock — are represented today.

Some of the preserved locomotives led charmed lives, such as No 24032. This had been sold to a scrap yard in Stockton-on-Tees and ran to the yard under its own power in July 1976, and would have been scrapped. However, at the same time the North Yorkshire Moors Railway suffered problems when its steam fleet had to be suspended due to the long hot summer of 1976 and an arrangement was quickly made (with the permission of BR) for the loan of the locomotive, initially for one year, but this was later extended when the railway leased the locomotive. Before being withdrawn for major repairs in 2001 the

locomotive had run 135,000 miles in preservation and was much valued by the Operating Department.

When No 25912, 25322 (D7672) was withdrawn in March 1987 it was sent to Leeds Holbeck shed the following month and became the responsibility of the Training Department based at York. It was overhauled by the apprentices and was able to work a number of rail tours. The locomotive had been repainted from its previous one-off livery (with yellow cabs and *Tamworth Castle* name) into two-tone green and renumbered back to D7672. Following its restoration by the apprentices in 1989 and formal naming as *Tamworth Castle* with cast plates, it was used on enthusiast specials until March 1991 when it was finally withdrawn and passed into preservation.

Similarly, No 25185 (D7535) had been retained at Toton depot for apprentice training following withdrawal in November 1984 and was finally disposed of in 1986, arriving at the Torbay & Dartmouth Railway in February of that year.

The preservation movement has performed minor miracles in keeping the class alive and working. At the time of withdrawal, these locomotives were worn out and suffering from major body corrosion, leaving the new owners and their support groups with a lot of work to do to return them to a good operating condition; they deserve your support.

| Class | Body style | Number | Current location | Status | Notes |
|---|---|---|---|---|---|
| 24/0 | Original | D5032, 24032 | North Yorkshire Moors Railway | Undergoing overhaul | Green, small warning panel |
| 24/1 | Original | D5054, 24054 | East Lancashire Railway | Operational | Green, no warning panel |
| 24/1 | Original | D5061, 24061, 97201 | North Yorkshire Moors Railway | Operational | Green, no warning panel |
| 24/1 | Original | D5081, 24081 | Gloucester Warwickshire Railway | Under repair | Blue |
| 25/1 | Original | D5185, 25035 | Great Central Railway | Operational | Green, no warning panel |
| 25/1 | Original | D5207, 25057 | North Norfolk Railway | Operational | Blue |
| 25/1 | Original | D5209, 25059 | Keighley & Worth Valley Railway | Under repair | Blue |
| 25/1 | Original | D5217, 25067 | Barrow Hill | Under restoration | Blue |
| 25/1 | Original | D5222, 25072 | Caledonian Railway | Under restoration | Blue |
| 25/2 | Revised | D5233, 25083 | Caledonian Railway | Undergoing overhaul | Stored in the open for 16 years before entering preservation. Blue |
| 25/3 | Revised | D7523, 25173 | West Somerset Railway | Operational | Two-tone green |
| 25/3 | Revised | D7535, 25185 | Paignton & Dartmouth Railway | Operational | Two-tone green |
| 25/3 | Revised | D7541, 25191 | North Yorkshire Moors Railway | Stored, awaiting restoration | Green, small warning panel |
| 25/2 | Original | D7585, 25235 | Bo'ness & Kinneil Railway | Under repair | Blue |
| 25/2 | Original | D7594, 25244 | Kent & East Sussex Railway | Stored. Has never run in preservation | In extremely poor condition with the body now green from mould. Requires major engine and generator repairs |
| 25/3 | Revised | D7612, 25262, 25901 | South Devon Railway | Operational | Blue |
| 25/3 | Revised | D7615, 25265 | Great Central Railway | Operational | Blue |
| 25/3 | Revised | D7628, 25278 | North Yorkshire Moors Railway | Under repair | Two-tone green |
| 25/3 | Revised | D7629, 25279 | Great Central Railway (Nottingham) | Operational | Two-tone green |
| 25/3 | Revised | D7633, 25283, 25904 | Dean Forest Railway | Undergoing restoration | Green |
| 25/3 | Revised | D7659, 25309, 25909 | Bo'ness & Kinneil Railway | Undergoing restoration | Green |
| 25/3 | Revised | 7663, 25313 | Llangollen Railway | Operational | Blue |
| 25/3 | Revised | D7671, 25321 | Midland Railway — Butterley | Operational | Owned by Derby Industrial Museum. Blue |
| 25/3 | Revised | D7672, 25322, 25912 | Churnet Valley Railway | Stored | Two-tone green |

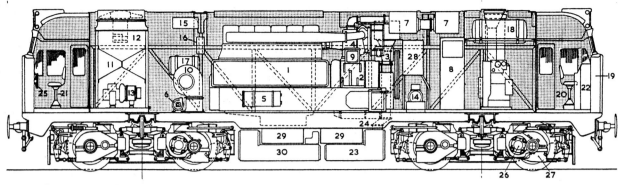

| 1 | Sulzer 6LDA28 diesel engine | 11 | Radiator | 21 | Assistant's seat |
|---|---|---|---|---|---|
| 2 | Main generator | 12 | Radiator fan and motor | 22 | Driver's controller |
| 3 | Exciter | 13 | Exhausters | 23 | Water Tank, 450gal |
| 4 | Pressure charger | 14 | Compressor | 24 | Water tank duct |
| 5 | Lubricating oil filter | 15 | Auxilliary fueland water tank | 25 | Handbrake |
| 6 | Fuel, oil and water pumps | 16 | Engine instrument panel | 26 | Traction motors |
| 7 | Engine silencer | 17 | Control reservoir | 27 | Reduction gear case |
| 8 | Electrical cubicle | 18 | Main reservoir | 28 | Brake gear cubicle |
| 8 | Voltage regulator | 19 | Flexible gangway | 29 | Batterybox |
| 10 | Motor blower set | 20 | Driver's seat | 30 | Fuel Tank |

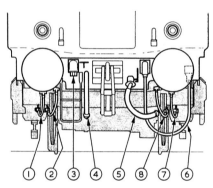

| 1 | Engine control pipe | 5 | Steam pipe |
|---|---|---|---|
| 2 | Main reservoir pipe | 6 | control jumper cable |
| 3 | Coupler socket | 7 | Engine control pipe |
| 4 | Vacuum pipe | 8 | Main reservoir pipe |

**No D5185 (25035) (Darlington 5/1963) has recently been overhauled on the GCR at Loughborough as is evident here by its smart green paintwork. The locomotive is fitted with the revised sandboxes and this view also shows the recessed doors and the larger fixed-front section of the cab side windows.** *Author*

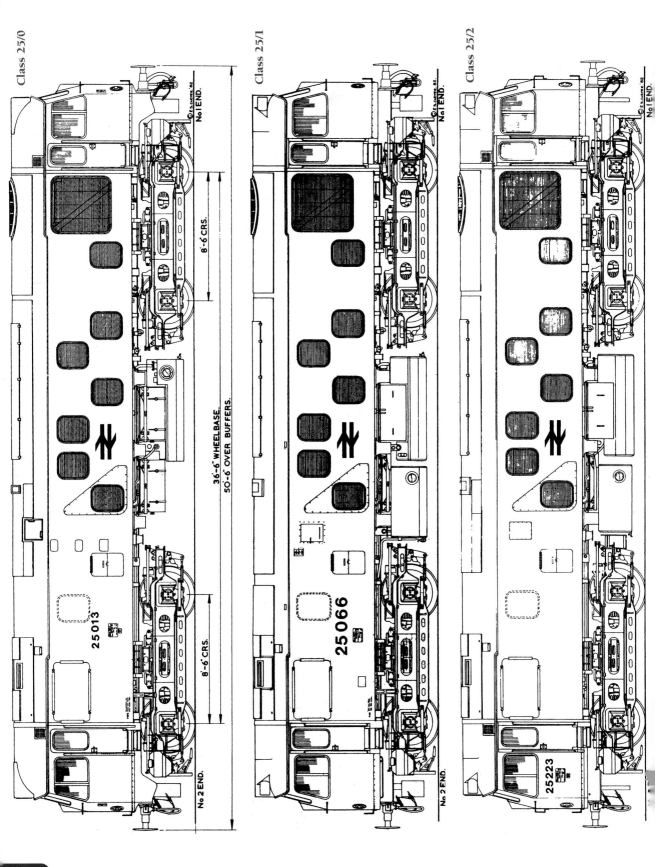

Class 25/0

Class 25/1

Class 25/2

No I END.

No I END.

No I END.

8'-6" CRS.

36'-6" WHEELBASE.
50'-6" OVER BUFFERS.

8'-6" CRS.

25013

25066

25223

No 2 END.

No 2 END.

No 2 END.

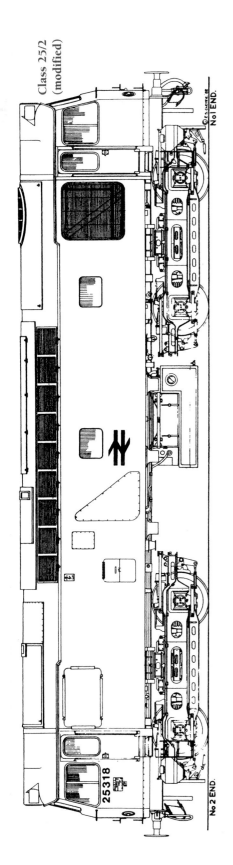

Class 25/2
(modified)

25318

No1 END.

No 2 END.

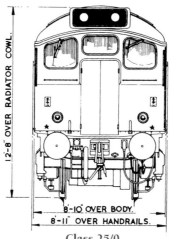

12'-8" OVER RADIATOR COWL.

8'-10" OVER BODY.

8'-11" OVER HANDRAILS.

**Class 25/0**

**Class 25/2**

**Class 25/1**

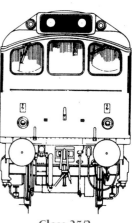

**Class 25/2**
**(modified)**